My Life

is a

Mystery

Mieke Benton

with Paul Benton

First Printing: June 2022
ISBN: 9798837014208

Contact the author at starshowerusa@startmail.com

Contents

Dedication

I dedicate this book to you, Paul, the sweetest, most gentle and honest man I know with very high integrity; and to our beautiful, intelligent and heart-based children, Andrew, Angela, and Christopher. The four of you gave my life value in ways I will never be able to express fully! Our reunion in this lifetime rekindled in me the universal truth of the inherent Divine in all of us.

I also dedicate this book to you, my Belgian family, my mom Anny, my dad Hugo (who still supports me from the afterlife), my brother Jeroen, my sister Leen and her son Gauthier. Thank you for your continuing love, respect and support.

Figure 1 Paul, Mieke, Andrew, Angela, Love, Christopher. Christmas 2008

Figure 2 Belgian American Family 2015. Paul, Andrew, Jeroen, Mieke, Anny, Gauthier, Angela, Leen, Christopher

Figure 3 Belgian American Family 2015

1. Introduction

Have you ever experienced any unusual things? Maybe you call them miracles or unexplained mysteries, or things people do not talk about? My life has been a series of mysteries. Some of them were so unusual that I didn't have any reference points to compare them. I kept those experiences in the back of my consciousness like a book I put back on the shelf to later pick up again.

The longer I live, the more those experiences start to have meaning, and the more I figure out why they are part of the mystery of my life and life in this universe. They didn't seem to be related to each other when they occurred, but now I see they do. Piece by piece, I am putting the puzzle together. I have always loved doing puzzles, and this one, my life, is truly my favorite! By connecting the dots, understanding occurs, and truth becomes revealed. All these experiences are part of a larger story; a vast reality about life in all its forms, it's about consciousness, about humanity's existence and beyond. You and I and everyone else are part of this story; we all play our own significant and unique role in this tapestry of life.

I have always wondered who am I, why am I here, and what is my life all about? When I pay attention to details and the bigger picture and use my discerning mind to put the pieces together, I see that there is meaning to my life and a reason for everything.

For as long as I remember, I have experienced very unusual things. To name here a few, who applied the brakes on my bike and prevented me from being hit by a sports car at age 11? Why am I just now getting more clarity about those moments of contact with extraterrestrials or inter-dimensional beings as a child, and why wouldn't my parents acknowledge my experiences? Why do some diseased people and animals I know come to me with messages? Why did my head turn to the left by itself just in time to see a spacecraft shoot into a 90-degree angle and disappear?

Besides the fact that I experienced those things and many more, it was even as strange that nobody else seemed to share similar things, or at least nobody was talking about it. Everyone seemed to be living their daily, agreed-upon "normal lives" and had no desire to question or discuss the unexplainable. What I experienced was labeled "just a dream" or "not true." So, what does one do in light of this? What if others don't believe you, laugh at you, or call you crazy? There was no place to talk about these things, so I kept them to myself. Maybe you recall some of these moments yourself in your life!

At age 51 (September 2021), I decided to put my experiences and insights in words and share them with the world. You might believe me or not, and I know that others might judge me. I understand that. It is wise to be discerning and not accept anything blindly if it is not experienced firsthand by yourself. My experiences are proof to me. I have nothing to prove to anyone, only a desire to understand my own experiences and make sense of it all. In the first place, I am writing for myself. It validates my life and acknowledges the things I have lived. But being able to honestly and openly share with others and communicate about it is what truly brings me joy, inner freedom, and peace.

Everyone has their own unique experiences and life lessons learned. When I share what I have lived, it might inspire others to share their own stories or realize that it is possible and OK to talk about them.

2. Who is Mieke Benton?

My name is Mieke Benton. I was born in Belgium in the city of Gent on September 3, 1970. My parents are Anny and Hugo De Clercq. I am the oldest of three children. Jeroen and Leen are my younger siblings. My grandparents opened a bookstore and a publishing company which later on, my parents took over the bookstore. Books and writing have always been a significant part of my life.

Figure 4 Mieke 1975

Figure 5 Mieke 2017

Figure 6 Mieke's Family 1974

Figure 7 Leen in Hood River, Oregon 2009

Figure 8 Jeroen and Paul, Bend, Oregon

Figure 9 Leen's son Gauthier, 2007

Even with all those books at my fingertips, I couldn't find the answers to the big questions I had been asking myself since a very young age - Who am I, What am I, Where did I come from, What is my purpose here? I was determined to find those answers.

I started school at two and a half years old in the Belgian school system. As one can imagine is very early to be removed from a loving home environment.

On my very first school day, my parents and grandparents drove me to school and left me behind for the first time in a foreign environment. They guided me to Martine, the teacher, and when I was distracted, they quickly left. When I noticed my family members were gone, I approached Martine and asked: "Do you have a car?" "Yes," she answered curiously. "I do have a car. Why do you want to know?" I replied, "Can you please take me home?"

I felt lost, and when I noticed I was left alone, I started looking for a solution. In my 2.5-year-old logic, I came with a car and needed to find a vehicle to get back home. My parents were gone, so I needed to find an adult in charge who could drive me back home.

This quest for home is still alive in me. I realize now that my true home is my inner connection with the source of all that is. There is a feeling of "beingness" in that connection - a deeper knowing of who and what I am. I know now that I am more than my body and personality. I know I am a divine multi-dimensional being, connected and part of the divine source. With that realization, I can finally come home.

In my teens, my grandfather told me how profound it was that I always made sure my younger brother and sister felt safe when I was a small child myself. He said, "You were always protecting them. You had such an extreme sense of responsibility, which was unusual at such a young age."

I do remember that feeling of over-responsibility. It was because I didn't always feel safe in this world and wanted to make sure my little brother and sister felt safe and protected.

This unsafe feeling and the inquiry from a very young age into the mysteries of life developed within me because I encountered situations and realities that extended far beyond this three-dimensional, physical world that I perceived with my five senses.

Because of these experiences, there are some things I know for sure. There are other worlds besides this one I live on. Other beings besides humans visit or live on the Earth.

Some of these encounters with other beings that were not human were benevolent and loving and other encounters terrified me because I didn't have a reference point, and I didn't understand it at such a young age. Those experiences showed me that there was vastly more to the story of my daily reality than my parents and society had told me. I wanted to make sense of it all.

A BIG question is how humans and extra-terrestrials are related and fit together in this planet's history. A thousand more unanswered questions are showing up for every question I pose. There is more that I don't know than there is that I do know.

I intend to share what I experienced. That's all that I do know for sure.

3. Family Traits

It wasn't that I was utterly alone in my unusual experiences. Several clues showed me that my parents and grandparents were in tune with nature and the energetic and paranormal world.

My parents were into alternative healing. We used homeopathy when we were sick, and under the guidance of our alternative house doctor, our family learned self-hypnosis breathing exercises as a way to relax. My mom still uses those techniques to go to sleep every night. My dad was almost blind and was the parent cooking and taking care of the children and household when we were at home, while my mom ran the book store, took care of the garden and did all the driving. My dad used all kinds of herbs from our garden while cooking. My parents reversed the usual male/female roles and tasks in my family.

My grandfather, who lived with us, created a large vegetable garden that provided many vegetables for the family and the neighbors. He was always observing nature, the weather, the animals, and the patterns in the sky. He was interested in the cosmos and was looking for answers about the universe's origin. He even joined the astronomy club. I wonder if he has seen UFOs in the sky. He never told me. I realize now that he knew about the cabal and the systems in society that we're going against humanity and nature. He knew more than he was supposed to know. Because of that, they labeled him schizophrenic, and they treated him with electro shocks. He threw his television out when I was a kid, and he didn't believe in "big pharma"; the pharmaceutical companies and practices. He had seen enough of the deceit of the system. He didn't want to go to doctors or dentists and build his own dentures out of metal. He dried grass and added that to his food. Looking back at it now, I see my grandfather as a shaman. He taught me to think for myself, work with nature, not be a sheeple in society, see the bigger picture in life, and become aware of the mind control techniques used on humanity.

Figure 10 Grandfather Pol & Mieke 1974

Figure 11 Grandfather Pol working his garden

My grandmother showed me since I was a very young child that if she lost an item, she called upon her deceased mother to help her find what she had lost. That often happened because she only had one seeing eye, which wasn't perfect either.

She demonstrated to me how she called upon her deceased mom; then, somebody unseen guided her to the lost item in no time. She had no idea where she was heading; my grandmother just walked, her hand went to the object, she picked it up and had the lost item in her hand. I have seen her do it many times, and she always told me, you can do that as well. Try it.

When I was 12 years young, I lost the wooden cross that I was supposed to wear around my neck on my second communion. A ritual in the Catholic Church that every 12-year-old has to attend through school. The whole family searched for a long time. We could not locate the cross, but we needed to go soon, or we would be late. I decided to use my grandmother's trick. I called upon her mother and asked her to help me find it. I walked towards a chair, picked up the bunch of clothes on that chair, and there it was. The cross we were looking for. "Found it," I yelled out loud. My experiment was proof that it worked, and I could use it when I needed it.

I have been using this technique since and still use it when I or anyone else loses something. I learned since then to set a time frame in which I want to find it, so it doesn't show up much later than I need it. I say, please can you help me find this in three minutes. Sometimes I say, please let me find it in the next five minutes if it is in the house. If I do not see it in those five minutes, it is not in the house. I learned to play with it.

I encourage others to use this technique. We can call those we know beyond the veil to help us find things.

My grandmother believed in communication with the afterlife and knew we could work together beyond the veil. She also told me something that most people will find hard to believe. I know from my intuition that she didn't make this up. She repeated it to me quietly a few times during my childhood. As if she was finding trust in me to share her experience. I just listened and found it very interesting what she shared.

My dad's older sister Caecilia was blind; she was born without any eyeballs. Mentally she remained at a 5-year-old level. She resided most of her life in institutions and came home on weekends.

Figure 12 Grandmother Maria, her blind daughter Caecilia, Mieke and her younger brother Jeroen 1972

My grandmother confided in me that someone told her about a secret section in the institution-building. Because of the people she knew, she was allowed into that hidden section. There she witnessed a human body with a bird's head. The only question I asked her was, "why do you say it had a bird's head?" Upon which she answered: "Because it had a beak." She didn't say

12

anything more than that. I just listened. I believe her because she shared it with me a handful of times during my childhood and teenage years. Especially now that I am aware of the many experiments happening with different species, I believe she witnessed something hidden from the public's eye. I know there is so much more going on than what the public has been aware of. I am thankful that she trusted me with this information.

To experience certain things, I believe we choose the family we are born into. I always wondered why I was born in a family with unusual disabilities such as no eyeballs, tiny eyeballs, blind and musically gifted people. Several of my family members have a highly developed intuition and have a keen perception of life and reality. It made me pay attention and questions even more "Who am I, What am I, Where am I, and Why am I here?"

Although my parents and grandparents showed me that there was more to life than most people are aware of, I still found it challenging to communicate what I was experiencing with them. Some experiences were so extraordinary that I and those around me could find no common reference point. I never blamed any of them for not being there for me in times of need. But it would have made my life much easier if I could have explored my experiences with someone who listened and acknowledged that what I was experiencing was real. Validation would have supported moving forward in life in a more balanced and fearless way.

4. Alien Abduction Experiences - What are they really?

These experiences are difficult to share and may be difficult for the reader to accept. I have no physical evidence that these occurrences happened, except they remain carved in my memory, feelings, and awareness. They influenced and challenged every aspect of my life and continue to do so up to this day.

Most of those early encounters that I consciously recall was taking place while living in the house my parents built in Deinze, in Belgium. They started around the time I started school at age two and a half in 1972.

What I remember are snapshots and glimpses. I only retained flashes of memories when coming out of those encounters. Comparable with when I wake up from a dream where the memories disappear very fast when I wake up. These experiences were obvious no dreams!

I remember being taken to a place, a room, completely foreign to me. I felt myself lying down naked on a cold metal table. It was extremely uncomfortable, and I could not move. I was lying on my back, looking up. I could only see what came into my view above me. Alien insect-like creatures with long stalky arms with three claw-like fingers were moving above me. They were looking at me. I could see their heads, arms with claws, and upper bodies. Their claws were moving above my body and poking, prodding into my body like surgical instruments. I was terrified and felt paralyzed from fear.

The closest comparison I can make of those beings with anything from here on earth would be a praying mantis; their arms and bodies moved in a choppy way. Their heads were triangle shaped. Their movements were not human-like.

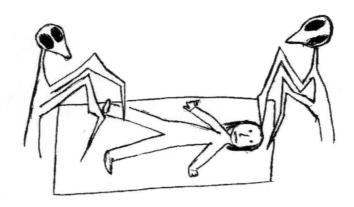

Figure 13 Alien Operatives

I sensed other smaller beings around me that I did not see. They were moving around lower than the table I was lying on. Those were not directly interacting with me.

Two of the three beings above me seemed to be in charge. They were standing at the head of the table I was lying on. They were leaning over me, observing me, and doing things with my body. This experience was nothing like anything I have ever experienced in my daily conscious life. They acted more like doctors, surgeons, or scientists.

I felt completely powerless and terrified, paralyzed by fear, unable to move. I was there all by myself, without parents or other humans. Nothing of my everyday human life was presented and related in that scenario. I felt myself entirely under their control and power and mortified to the bone.

I came out of these foreign experiences with a deep feeling of terror. Suddenly, I experienced myself back in my bed at home. Those flashes of memory of where I just came from made me aware of what just had happened. Extremely terrified, I opened my eyes and saw my bedroom.

In total terror, afraid to scream for my parents to come to my room, I strategized what to do next. I considered all my options. Do I feel brave enough to run towards my parent's bedroom and get in bed with them where I feel safe? I often did not choose that option out of fear to run through the dark hallway because I knew there were energy-beings present in the hallway that didn't feel good. Shall I scream for my parents in the hope they will hear me and come to my room? Sometimes I decided to scream for my parents, and no sound came out of my mouth, making it even more terrifying. Shall I stay in bed, hide under my sheets and think very fast and loud to distract myself away from those memories and hope that I will quickly fall asleep? But what if I go back into the same situation, I wondered, which happened before. Sometimes I immediately was retaken into the same room. I knew it was possible.

Every time I came out of one of those experiences, I had to make a decision and felt like I had to make it fast, almost like a life-or-death situation.

Those experiences, as described above, continued to occur into my teenage years in that same bedroom—the total amount of those experiences I do not consciously recall. To the best of my recollection, it happened more often when I was younger and once in my puberty, at least once every two years. Most likely, it happened more often.

Sometimes I was fully conscious while being in the process of entering back into my body in my bed at home. I was aware that I was back in my body, but I couldn't move my body yet. It felt like the connection was not activated yet. It was a scary feeling not having control over my body vehicle. I experienced this process of trying to make the connection, and it not working, as a struggle. First, I tried to move my head to the left, no luck, no movement. Then I tried to move my head to the right, still no action, then I tried to push back to the left. I kept trying and forcing it, with no prevail, no movement. It was scary, frightening, and frustrating at the same time. Until suddenly, something kicked in. Without warning and with a shock, I first moved my head again and then the rest of my body. After having experienced this on several occasions, I learned that if I patiently waited a little bit without going into fear, I would soon be able to move my body again. I learned from experience not to freak out, wait, and allow the movement to come back.

Despite those unexplainable terrifying, and confusing experiences, what was even more devastating, was that my parents couldn't grasp what I was going through; they were clueless.

Finally, I reached my parents by screaming or running towards their room; their response was the opposite of what I needed at that moment. But how could they know what I just went through?

They wanted to soothe me by telling me it was just a dream, a nightmare. My parents tried to help me let go of the scary thoughts and feelings to go back to bed and sleep. They weren't aware of the terror I was in or what I had just experienced. They always said it was just a dream; it is over now. I was terrified to go back to sleep, knowing that sometimes I would be abducted again.

After going through several of those occurrences at a very young age, my dad tried to figure out why I was so afraid. He thought maybe it was the wallpaper in my bedroom with Little Red Riding Hood and the Big Angry Wolf that scared me and gave me nightmares. I remember him asking me if it was the wolf that frightened me. The wolf picture on the wallpaper was nothing compared to the alive insect creatures I had just encountered, but I could not express all of that; I was too young. One day, they changed my wallpaper, thinking that might help. My parents didn't know what was happening to me. They had no idea why I was so scared. They were taking care of three young children the best they could in a loving and supportive way.

Now I realize that this little child in me, the teenager and young adult inside myself, were never validated for their experiences. I have been living with that terror inside and without an explanation for why I felt that way. That deep feeling of fear and vulnerability stayed with me.

At age 28, I met my husband Paul and later also others who experienced extraterrestrial encounters. Paul and I didn't know till much later into our marriage that we both had encounters. Paul's encounters were all positive. I had both benevolent and what seemed to be malevolent encounters. I questioned why I had experiences that created so much fear in me. Finally, for the first time, into my thirty's, somebody acknowledged my experiences. A deep layer of terror that I had been carrying for most of my life started to dismantle. I wasn't alone anymore. I could discuss it with others, and my experiences made more sense. I learned that listening to what other people are experiencing is very important, regardless of their age or situation. It might not be my reality, but it is authentic for them.

I always listen intently when children and adults are telling me about their unusual experiences, their dreams, or talk about their invisible friends. I acknowledge and validate their experiences; no matter how extra-ordinary those stories may seem. Many phenomena don't have an accepted explanation yet.

Those experiences influenced all parts of my life. By sharing openly and honestly, I might plant a seed for others to do the same. In doing so, we can create more clarity about what is really going on and transform our fears, anxieties, terror, confusion, and isolation and start living a more relaxed, open, connected, united and joyous life.

Afternote:

As I live my life, there are always more questions than answers. I realize that I have had benevolent ET experiences where only love is involved and no fear. And then I had those terrifying abduction experiences, that do not make sense to me, they create more confusion and bring up more questions. From doing my investigation, I come to believe that my terrifying abduction experiences are most likely related to Military Abduction Projects, also known as MILAB programs. More and more information is coming out about those secret mind control projects, to name here a few: Project Paperclip, Project Montauk, Project Moonstruck, MK Ultra (=Project Bluebird = Project Artichoke), Project Orion, MK-Delta, Project Stargate, Project Bluebeam etc; it goes on and on. I do not know much about those programs, I just know they exist, at least since the 1950's and have been kept secret from the general public. They have been used in all parts of our society and influenced and controlled our minds and emotions without most people knowing about it.

What also has been kept secret for a very long time is the hidden military arsenal of highly advanced technology. Star Wars Technology does exist on this planet at this time. These advanced anti-gravity craft are back engineered by humans from E.T. technology. It is important that we the people are informed about this so that no False-Flag Alien Space War created by human hands can fear and scare us. Like anything else, anti-gravity and other quantum technology can be used and applied to create good for humanity or to create more fear and control of humanity. When we are informed, we can choose to make wiser choices this time around. This powerful technology can be used for our highest good, it can create many solutions for our transportation needs, energy generation, medical healing applications and other peaceful uses.

This hidden technology has been used for more than 75 years, unfortunately by the wrong hands. It is about time that those "greedy and selfish people" be exposed and handled with. Humanity can handle the truth and wants to be set free!

I do not have proof that I was part of those projects. As time goes by and more people share their piece of the puzzle, ultimately the truth will be revealed. I am contributing my piece of the puzzle by sharing what I do remember I have experienced myself.

Another pattern I recognize is the sizzling sound in my ears and head right before a less benevolent encounter is about to happen.

I trust the unfolding of my life. The answers will appear when I am ready for them.

5. Invisible Hand

My parents longed for a place of their own to call home and raise their children, a domain with privacy to do what they wanted without my grandmother's overseeing, controlling eye. With the help of family members and friends, they built their own beautiful home. We called it "Leieland" after the street name, Leiepark and the Leie, the river passing by. My mom was six months pregnant with my sister Kathleen and wanted to move into the house before the birth. We moved in around Easter 1973. I was then two and a half years old and my brother nine months old.

It was an excellent place for us kids to grow up. The home was built in a cul-de-sac with no through traffic. We freely played in the street with many neighborhood children until late at night. Behind our house were grass field pastures with cows and a pond, a perfect environment to connect with nature and learn valuable life lessons! My mom was usually very busy at our bookstore in town, and my vision impaired dad accompanied her or stayed at home with us kids and the many animals. At times it looked like an animal farm. We had a dog, a donkey, peacocks, sheep, goats, chickens, rabbits, birds, and a cat, which kept our domain full of life.

I loved the freedom I had to ride my bike from our house to the bookstore and back, which was about a 15-minute bike ride.

On one of those trips, something extraordinary happened. It was the summer of 1981; I was 11 years old. It was a beautiful day. I took my bike out of the garage and headed to our bookstore. Peacefully I biked through the Machelenstraat, which connected our street, Leiepark, with the major thoroughfare. There were no traffic lights there in 1981, which would not be possible today.

I was about to cross the four-lane thoroughfare and looked for cars coming from each direction. I had made this crossing safely many times. I first looked to the left for upcoming traffic. I didn't see any cars coming my way, and I peddled to the left turn lane and stopped. Then I looked for oncoming traffic from the right coming in my direction. I saw a red car in the far distance but decided it was still far away. I figured there was plenty of time for me to cross. I mounted the seat and started peddling. I didn't realize as an eleven-year-old that it was a red sports car approaching me at full speed. I was peddling and focused on where I was going and wasn't paying attention to the vehicle anymore.

Now I was in the middle of the two lanes with the sports car approaching me at high speed. I had no idea. I truly wasn't prepared for what was to come next!

Suddenly, the brakes of my bike were engaging by themselves. Completely to my surprise, my bike stopped abruptly. I almost flew over my handlebars. The red sports car zoomed by about an inch in front of me at the exact moment. I heard the sound of a speeding car passing by and saw a blur of red in front of me.

Then I found myself with feet solidly on the ground and my hands firmly holding the handlebars. I was utterly baffled. I knew at that moment that some invisible intervention had taken place. If it hadn't, I would have been dead. This intervention was beyond my comprehension. I was still alive, and I shouldn't have been I remember speaking aloud. Clearly, I remember thinking to myself, "hum, well, it is clear that it is not my time to die. I must still be alive for a specific reason. I wonder what's important in my future because I should be dead now." I became quiet inside. What just happened?

I took a deep breath. I was curious if my brakes would still be engaged or not. They were not. When the road was safe to cross, I mounted my bike again and peddled a few seconds later. I drove to the bookstore in inner silence, totally stunned by what had just happened. I knew in that instance that this was a significant event in my life.

As I entered the bookstore, I saw my mom behind the counter serving customers. I patiently waited till the line of customers had disappeared, and she had a moment to herself without distractions. I calmly told her what had just happened. She looked at me. I could see she was trying to comprehend what I told her, but then more customers arrived at the counter, and she was consumed again in her work. How could she possibly comprehend this anyway, I thought to myself? I didn't even understand what had just happened! I did realize that it was an extremely out-of-the-ordinary experience. An invisible hand had intervened in the stream of my life, and it had saved my life. Somehow it wasn't my time to die! I got the message.

About two weeks later, I rode my bike again on that same road. I was nearly half a mile further down and over a bridge this time. There was another crossroad, only smaller. A car was parked with the front windshield completely shattered on the roadside. There had recently been a severe accident. I still saw bloodstains on the ground and some pieces of glass were still present. As I approached that car closer and observed the broken front windshield, I saw a chunk of long blond hair stuck in the broken, shattered windshield. I stopped my bike and thought, "this could have been my hair. It could have been me." Some other girl was less lucky than me. She most likely died, and I am still alive.

The intervention that I had experienced a few weeks earlier was brought clearly into my awareness again. I felt grateful that I was still alive. It also raised many more questions. Who or what was it that saved my life?

6. The Movie E.T. - The Extra-Terrestrial

It was November 1982. I was twelve years old, and the movie E.T. premiered in the Belgian movie theaters. My mom unexpectedly asked if we wanted to see the film with her. My brother and sister, and I eagerly agreed. Going with my mom to the movie theater didn't happen often. She was working in our bookstore most of the time and was the only parent that could drive the car. My dad was born almost blind, and the eyesight on his one seeing eye was not able to see a movie on the big screen. Most films were spoken in English, which he could understand, but the Dutch subtitles were invisible. Even sitting in the front row, he couldn't see anything. The fact that my mom was taking us to the movies was a miracle in itself.

Excited, we arrived at the Decascoop, the then just renovated fancy movie theatre in Gent, about a 20-minute drive from our hometown, Deinze. As the four of us settled comfortably into the theater chairs, the movie started rolling.

As a side note, by the age of 12, I had experienced several alien abductions in my young life. The memory flashes and feelings were always immediately erased and gone before I got out of bed in the morning. While watching that movie, I had no conscious recollection of any abduction experiences or contact with extra-terrestrials.

Watching the big screen, I became completely immersed in the movie. What captured me the most was that the other aliens left E.T. behind on Earth. I felt empathy for E.T. and felt his abandonment deeply inside of me. He was such a loving and sensitive creature. How would he survive in a world so harsh and uncaring as ours? I was intrigued and captured by the story but not prepared for what would happen to me during the last minutes of the movie.

The spaceship finally answered E.T.'s call and came back to pick him up. I noticed that while E.T. was standing near the spacecraft, his heart was glowing. He said goodbye to Michael and Gertie, who held the chrysanthemum that E.T. had revived. Before he boarded the spaceship, he told Elliott, "I'll be right here," pointing his glowing finger to Elliott's forehead. He then picked up the flower, got onto the spaceship, and it took off, leaving a beautiful rainbow trail in the sky. All actors in the movie and all of us in the movie theater watched intently. He was able to GO HOME. I was so relieved!

Then without warning, a heavy sadness welds up from deep inside me. My heart fell into the most profound sadness I had ever experienced. I sobbed uncontrollably and couldn't stop. I kept crying and crying and crying. I remember falling into my mom's lap. She told me to stop, and I couldn't. It was beyond my control.

The movie was over. The credits came and ended. I kept sobbing, and my mom guided me to the car. I remember riding in the car, observing myself in this state of sadness, and at the same time wondering why I was crying so hard. It didn't make sense to my logical mind. It was interesting that I was having these feelings, and at the same time, I was able to observe myself and be in the wonder of it all. Why was I doing this? I asked myself.

By the time we got home, my crying had stopped, but I was still in wonder why I responded like that. How could I be so profoundly emotionally affected by the events at the end of that movie? And why was I not able to control my emotions? It didn't make any sense to me.

7. What Happens After the Body Dies?

My grandmother, Elza Cozijns, my mom's mom, died from cancer when I was 20 years old. I clearly remember her last day. My mom and I were with her at the hospital. The whole time my mom was holding her mother's hand while I was sitting next to the bed observing everything. It was so beautiful and powerful to see and experience this very intimate encounter between them. I admired my mom's strength.

At one moment, my mom said, "I need to go to the bathroom. Can you take over? Just hold her hand and talk to her". I felt a little insecure at that moment. I had never held my grandma's hand in such an intimate way. Totally out of my comfort zone, I did what my mom had asked me to do.

I felt my dying grandmother's fragile small, wrinkled hand within my hand and talked to her. She opened her eyes, smiled at me, and expressed one of her silly faces with which I was very familiar. Deeply touched, I looked into her eyes and smiled back.

A little later, someone came to pick me up and brought me home while my mom stayed at my grandma's bedside during the night. A priest came to give her the last sacraments in the night, making my grandma very happy. After that, she got more morphine for the pain and didn't wake up for the rest of the night. My mom's youngest sister stayed at her bedside in the morning, and my mom went home. Leaving the hospital that morning, my mom knew that this was the last time she would see her mom. Fifteen minutes later, my grandmother had died.

The night after my grandmother's funeral, I noticed a white shimmer in the hallway and became curious about what that was. It looked like someone was standing there with a white sheet over themselves. I had a sense that I knew who it was and curiously asked, "grandma, is that you?".

Slowly she pulled the white sheet away from herself and confirmed enthusiastically, "yes, it is me!" My grandmother stood about 15 feet (5 meters) away from me in the dark hallway, totally illuminated.

I was extremely excited that I had another chance to see her again because she just had died. I was thrilled that I could communicate with her and that she was answering my questions. I had so many questions and was full of excitement while firing them off. "Are you back together with grandpa now?" I eagerly asked her. In a peaceful, content, and satisfying tone, she said, "yes, we are back together now." I felt how relaxed she was to be reunited again with my grandfather. Next I thought, "maybe she can see my favorite poodle dog, Joepie, again, who had passed away a year earlier." Excitingly, I asked, "what about Joepie - do you seen him?" "No, he is not here with me, but he is here somewhere."

She transferred to me her feeling of deep inner peace. I felt how delighted and free she felt, which was undoubtedly the most incredible feeling she transmitted - beyond words to explain! I sensed a deep feeling of centeredness and authentic power in her.

Then she told me that she wanted me and everyone else to know that there was no need to grieve. Death wasn't what we thought it was. She explained when people die and leave their bodies and life on Earth; they reunite with those they loved and who crossed over before them. She wanted to clarify that it is not necessary to spend any time grieving. She explained that if we knew that those who passed are fine and happy and free, we would be pleased about it ourselves. She said that grieving is absolutely unnecessary and a waste of our precious time.

I wanted to ask lots more questions because I was so excited and curious, but she said she had to go. I understood.

My grandma Elza slowly faded away and was gone. I felt so good and empowered and happy to have had that experience and know how she felt. It gave me a deep sense of inner peace, and I knew at that moment that death is not something to fear or resist. I knew then that what we have been told about death is not true.

The following day, I was eager to share my powerful experience with my mom. She had to know the news about her mom and the message that no grieving was necessary.

My mom was sitting at the kitchen table, and I immediately expressed my joyful and empowering experience and the message her mom had for all of us - not to grieve. I think my mom was in grief. She heard me and responded to what I said, but I do not know how much of what I said she was able to feel and receive.

I felt a wave of profound inner peace. I can still feel the peace of that experience when I think about that moment. Since then, I have known that death is not what most humans think. I am not afraid of it anymore. There is so much more to life and death than what we have been told and shown.

Death, dying, and the afterlife have always been fascinating subjects. Since my grandmother died, I have helped several people cross over; and on several occasions, I was the last person with them before they let go. I saw them responding in bliss right before they left. Their face lit up, and they relaxed. A beautiful smile emerged directly before they passed.

I also spent time in funeral homes with the deceased bodies of friends who had killed themselves. In those situations, I could see the pain they had acquired in their lives stored in those bodies. I could sense the distress on their faces.

I learned that a soul hangs around their bodies immediately after a person dies. The soul is first learning to figure out what just happened. I can feel and sense their souls still hanging in the room, and they know I can feel them. I always talk to the deceased one. Dying is a process we learn from, as is life. We learn from all our experiences.

There is so much more to life and death than we know. It doesn't end with death. There is a new unfolding after that. Our awareness does not stop when we leave our earthly bodies. We breathe in our last breath. We breathe it out, and we move on.

Figure 14 Grandparents Albert & Elza, Leen, Jeroen & Mieke 1973

8. Out-of-Body Experiences, Astral Travel, Lucid Dreaming and Remote Viewing

Out-of-body experiences, astral travel, lucid dreaming, and remote viewing are innate human abilities. It is part of who we are. Those human attributes were mentioned and talked about during all ages of history.

For example, every night when I go to sleep, my spirit leaves my physical body and travels into other dimensions. While somehow, I stay connected to my body. I don't remember this when I wake up most of the time. We can also use these innate abilities when we are awake, practice them at will, and use those with intent and purpose.

I have consciously experienced several of these occurrences and often remembered them when I returned to my awake state.

Most of the time, those experiences happened to me unexpectedly. At other times, I was able to leave my body at will. I remained conscious during the experience and upon my return to my body.

I realized early in my life that being in a physical body can feel very dense and limited, which contrasts with out-of-body experiences where my spirit can move around freely in different dimensions and locations without the constraints of my body.

There is lots of information available about out-of-body experiences, astral travel, lucid dreaming, and remote viewing. I personally do not want to label them in different boxes. There are some differences in my experience, but they can also blend together and overlap each other.

From a very early age, I remember having out-of-body experiences. I called those my flying dreams. They were always very delightful to me. Sometimes I took off in a flash, flying away from my body. Sometimes it started in a dream as a jumping session on a trampoline. I could feel myself soaring out of my body higher and higher with every jump I made until I found myself flying around freely. I could consciously choose wherever I wanted to go from that point on. I was flying without boundaries and could observe my earthly surroundings away from my physical body. I enjoyed those experiences. I was not consciously making this happen. It pleasantly surprised me when it did happen.

Then there were my astral traveling experiences. Those happened randomly and pleasantly surprised me when they occurred. Since moving to the United States, I have traveled a few times to my birth country, Belgium, this way, while my physical body remained asleep in bed. In those experiences, I was able to walk around on the streets I am very familiar with from when I lived there. I felt the energy of the place - the smells, the feel of the cobblestones under my feet, all the details of the buildings, the elements of nature, my interactions with friends and family, and the people on the street that were not aware of me. All my senses were involved as if I was there physically.

I enjoyed every second of it because I consciously knew that this experience would be short-lived. I encountered people I knew, and we were happy to see each other. On one occasion, I met a girlfriend that I knew from my past, which I had not consciously thought about since I last saw her when I was young. In that encounter, we were both astonished to see each other after so much time had passed. We were now older in that experience.

Then, upon awakening in my bed in California, I felt completely aligned and at peace, knowing that I had made the right decision to move to America, and I felt joyful that I had the opportunity to be in Belgium during that night. I had an actual visit, I didn't have to pay for a plane ticket, and it didn't take any travel time to get there and back—an in the present moment gratifying conscious full-body experience.

I have also experienced what is called lucid dreaming. In those dreams, I am consciously aware that I am dreaming. I am present in my dream; I can control every detail and create the dream the way I want it to be. I can make the others in my dream do what I want them to do. I can consciously change all the details of the dream in any way I desire at that moment. I have total control.

When I was 12 years of age and passionately in love with a boy in my town, I experienced a lucid dream. I created him in my dream and passionately desired him to kiss me. I was aware of my ability to make anything happen at will, and after a bit of consideration, I decided to let him kiss me. The fact that I could consciously design and direct my dream at that moment was fascinating, and what was even more exhilarating was the awareness that I could make him kiss me as if it were his own choice! When I woke up from this lucid dream, I stayed consciously aware of the experience and the control I had over it. I felt immensely disappointed that I had only been able to make him kiss me in my dream and not in real life!

On occasion, I have experienced remote viewing. I tapped into a location and could see what was going on there without being there. This experience happened at night when I was asleep, and I have practiced this while awake.

I know remote viewers who use this ability as a profession. They can access items, people, or locations to solve problems; they might access a crime scene or locate a missing person, and some have used this to find water, gold, or oil deposits. It can also be used to sense into the body and locate imbalances and disease processes. When remote viewing, locations, and time frames can be explored that are different from where the remote viewer is located him or herself.

As human beings, we have many magnificent innate abilities. Unfortunately, many of these have purposely been denied and withheld from us. What would happen if we openly discussed those abilities with each other and our young children or if we practiced those abilities in schools, workplaces, and at home? We would learn from each other and regain access to our incredible potentials and capabilities.

9. Nightly Procedure

In my sleep one night in 1996, I was visited again. I was 26 years old and living by myself in my tiny home in Deinze. The visitors I am talking about were not human.

My bed was located in the only upstairs room. I was lying on my stomach, and I noticed beings next to my bed. I knew and could feel that "they" were measuring my back. Who they were, I did not know? I noticed it was not one single entity. "They" were operating as a team.

They measured my back in exactly three equal parts. I am not sure if they had told me what they were doing. I felt it, and I knew. After taking the measurements, they pinpointed the first of the three parts, and very unexpectedly, they inserted something very sharp in that spot. It felt like a large needle. I jumped and made a frantic sound from the core of my being. It was excruciating, and it shocked me deeply.

I had no idea what they were doing, and before I even had time to figure it out, those beings located the second section of my back, and another insertion occurred—same procedure. Again, I responded in the same way. I felt an energetic shock in the depth of my being, and I voiced it.

There was no time to respond to what was happening. Before I could catch up with myself, a third insertion penetrated my body. Distressed and unwilling to handle one more insertion, I opened my eyes. What was that? Who were they? What was that all about? I knew something extraordinary had happened, and it wasn't a dream.

Before I could turn my body around in bed and sit up, they were gone.

During that time, I was enrolled in Psychodynamic classes in Centrum Gea in Belgium – an alternative healing center where we learned about consciousness, energies, and healing. The next evening in class, I decided to share what happened that previous night with Els, the teacher. I wanted some answers or someone I could share this experience with that I trusted. I knew Els would be open and not discount it, ridicule it, or label it as a dream or fantasy.

I shared with Els precisely what happened. Els responded, "Do you think their intent was benevolent or malevolent?" I gave myself a moment to feel into my impressions of this experience. I didn't feel any hostile intent. I told Els I concluded they most likely were benevolent.

Els said it appears to me that those beings don't have a human body with emotions and feelings, as we have. They have no idea how what they were doing feels and how much pain and discomfort they were causing you. You will have to let them know.

What Els said made sense to me. That evening when I came home from class, I mentally stated. "OK, guys! I am not sure who you are, but that procedure you were doing to me last night startled me and caused me great pain and discomfort. You have no idea what it is like to be in a human body. You will have to find a different approach that does not cause me discomfort whatever you are doing. Otherwise, I will not allow such action anymore."

Since then, I have not experienced any more painful occurrences. I know there have been more interactions since then. Somehow, I know that we are still connected and in contact with each other.

That experience taught me that it is utterly important to clearly communicate what I want and how the actions and words of others are affecting me, especially if it infringes on my sovereignty and free will.

I know that human beings are not the only species in the universe(s). Humans are equally as powerful and valuable as any other species in the tapestry of life. Claiming our human sovereignty and respecting the sovereignty of other species is the first step in a co-creation where everyone wins. A co-creation that supports the higher good of all involved.

10. Our Paths Coming Together

It became apparent to me. I needed to learn to live by myself. Through my teenage years and towards my mid-twenties, I had been in several long-term relationships. Being comfortable in my own presence was a challenge for me. At age 26, I was courageous enough to act upon this inner calling. With my golden retriever, Rayca, I was living in a small house with a garden in the town of Deinze in Belgium. I had a college degree in orthopedagogy and worked as a special education counselor in a facility with mentally and physically disabled adults.

Figure 15 My beautiful Golden Retriever Rayca

I was figuring out how to navigate in society and, at the same time, learning how to follow my own heart. Instead of looking for attention and validation in the outside world, I was called to look inside myself. Little by little, I permitted myself to do those things that were nurturing to my soul. Attending alternative healing classes in Centrum Gea was such a gift to me. There I was given more tools to expand my awareness and focus on the direction of my heart. I found a community of like-minded people who were on a similar path.

At the same time, Paul was on his journey of learning to listen to his own heart. Without knowing each other, we had the same intent. We both wanted to love ourselves and open our hearts to life authentically. Looking for another intimate relationship was not a priority for both of us at the time.

Figure 16 Paul

Paul will share in his own words a little about himself.

Paul: How do I begin to tell you what an amazing journey this is. Mieke and I came together or, more accurately, collided most unusually and magically. We were exploring what was true for each of us and what was important in life. What is the essence of living a life of meaning, joy, and purpose? What is love? The kind of love that sits at the base of a life worth living.

Figure 17 Paul and Mieke 2005

I was born in Hood River, Oregon, in 1949 and spent my early years living and working on a fruit orchard with my parents and four siblings. I was the middle child. After high school, I attended Oregon State University and graduated with a Bachelor of Science degree in pre-med. In 1972, I was admitted to the Oregon Health Sciences University. I graduated in 1976 with a Doctor of Medical Dentistry degree. I was in private dental practice until 1981. I left the practice of dentistry due to health reasons and due to a benevolent E.T. encounter that opened my eyes to the larger reality of which we are apart. This encounter sparked an interest in the study of frequencies and computers.

Figure 18 Baby Paul 1951

Figure 19 Paul 1961

Figure 20 Paul Highschool 1967

Figure 21 Paul 1980

This trail led me to San Francisco, where I studied computer programming and operations. I secured a job in the computer department at the University of the Pacific School of Dentistry. I was also an adjunct instructor teaching Comprehensive Patient Care. Shortly after that, I consulted with private practices helping them computerize their businesses—all of this while living in San Francisco.

Two marriages and three kids later, I found myself again living and working in Hood River.

Figure 22 Single dad Paul, Christopher, Andrew, Angela 1995

In 1995, I attended the East-West College of the Healing Arts and completed a course in massage therapy. I wanted to get as much experience as possible to start my new career. I asked around to find the best massage therapist in Portland. I got the name of Bob White from several sources, so I called him up to introduce myself. I asked Bob what the best way is to become proficient in massage therapy. He said, "put your hands on a thousand bodies." That excellent advice led me to become a pre-surgical massage therapist at the Mid-Columbia Medical Center in the Dalles. I also took Bob's Onsen Massage course and kept expanding my knowledge and experience.

Figure 23 Paul and his (twin brother) Bob White

Sometime in 1996, after Bob and I had become friends, he mentioned that I should meet Frank Coppieters, who was putting together a school at his Living Light Center in Portland. I could not see how I could add any more activities to my already hectic schedule at that time. Finally, I agreed to go to the introductory meeting for the new school, which was to be called The Practical School of Wisdom and Compassion. I met Frank and Marilyn there and quickly realized that this was the next phase in my alternative healing journey. I recognized that these two teachers embodied the highest essence of the divine masculine and the divine feminine. I wanted to take part in their creation. The Practical School of Wisdom and Compassion began in early 1997.

To take advantage of this unique opportunity, I would need to find a reliable and loving person to stay with the three kids while I attended Frank and Marilyn's school one evening a week in Portland. Fortunately, I found the perfect solution in my niece, Mandy Benton. The kids already knew Mandy and loved to be with her. It is impressive how the ideal solutions appear when I follow my heart on my life's journey.

Figure 24 Mandy, Andrew and Paul 2007

When Mieke and I met in 1998, I was a single parent of three young children, Christopher, three and a half years old, Angela, six, and Andrew, nine. I was working three jobs. One as a pre-surgical massage therapist at Mid-Columbia Medical Center in The Dalles. I had a private massage therapy practice in Hood River and taught Tai-Chi classes in The Dalles and Hood River. I was living moment to moment while at the same time trying to make some sense out of this existence. It was the most challenging time I had ever experienced. I cared for three small children full time, transported them to daycare and school, and provided for all their other needs.

Figure 25 Paul, Angela, Christopher at Crater Lake, OR 1997

Figure 26 Andrew, Angela, Christopher. Crater Lake 1998

Mieke: Hearing the announcement of the Oregon/Belgian retreat in my evening class in Belgium, I immediately felt ecstatic! I jumped to the front of my chair. Without giving it a thought, I put my hand in the air and said, "I am interested!" My heart spoke without waiting for my mind to kick in, which usually does not happen often!

As a 19-year-old, I had been an international exchange student in the USA. I worked two months in upstate New York in a camp for disabled children, followed by a month-long fantastic trip from New York all the way to the Keys in Florida and back up. Those three months in the USA had been the best time in my life so far.

When the opportunity arose to go to America again in combination with my passion, which was alternative healing, I quickly said to myself, "I do not know how I am going to make it work, but I am going!" This opportunity was a no-brainer; my heart was leading the way. I was 27 at the time.

The trip came together effortlessly and joyfully from the moment I had made that decision. It was as if the universal life source said, "Oh, you are clear on what you want? Let me help you get there in the most powerful and efficient way!

Paul: I first learned about the joint retreat with the Belgians at a class meeting with Frank and Marilyn. This would be a week-long international alternative healing experience with people from a completely different culture. I was intrigued by the possibilities of learning how similar or dissimilar the approaches to and healing modalities were.

I imagined us coming together from two disparate cultures with similar desires and approaches but was concerned about a possible language barrier. Would there be awkward interactions in our working and living customs? Would there be enough commonality to have a meaningful and productive exchange? In high school, the only foreign language I had taken was German, not Dutch. Frank eased my concern by stating that most Belgians spoke some English and that any communication challenges could be easily overcome.

I strongly wanted to attend this workshop with the Belgians but could not see how I could financially afford it. I struggled to meet the financial requirements of parenting and providing for my children and myself. I voiced my desire and concern with Frank and Marilyn.

After a week or two, Frank came up with a brilliant idea. If I were part of the childcare team, I could attend some workshop exercises and be in Breitenbush with my three children. This solution was a miracle! I could attend, and my three young children could come too. This was going to happen!

In July 1998, it all came together. Thirty Belgians flew over with four of their children and joined our American group that consisted of 25 Americans and four children, of which three were my own.

11. Synchronicities at Their Best

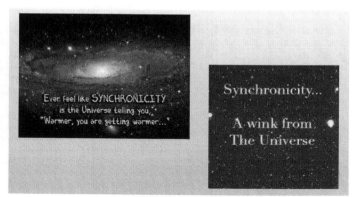

Figure 27 Synchronicity

Once the retreat started and over the next ten days when we Belgians explored Oregon on our own, powerful occurrences and synchronicities occurred between Paul and me. After a while, those events were boggling our minds. Miraculously, Paul and I reunited without intent in the most unexpected ways. We were astonished and didn't understand what was happening. Nothing made any logical sense.

By the time we Belgians were flying back to Belgium, Paul and I were confused. What is happening here? Nothing made sense to our rational minds. Remember, we were both NOT looking to get involved in a relationship.

A series of events made us question what was going on here.

Figure 28 Breitenbush Hotsprings 1998

11.1. Divinely Inspired Rendezvous

Our internationally combined group of Belgians and Americans was at Breitenbush Hot Springs retreat in Oregon. After breakfast, my Belgian roommate, Eliane, and I headed toward the showers in the bathhouse close to the cabins.

Walking down the stairs of the main lodge with satisfied bellies, we basked in the warm sunshine." Are we in heaven or what?" we proclaimed! Continuing our walk through the field toward the cabins, I noticed Paul and his three children walking a little bit further ahead of us.

As I observed the four of them, I turned to Eliane and said, "Eliane, do you see Paul there with his three children?" Eliane turned her gaze towards them. I continued: "Do you see how Paul is interacting with his children? So nurturing, calm, kind, loving, and patient." I noticed that Christopher, the youngest, was upset and not happy at all. Paul stopped, kneeled, checked in with his youngest while still holding his other kids by the hand. He lovingly talked to Christopher, which calmed him down, and in no time, they were all together hand in hand walking in peace toward the cabins. "Do you see that, Eliane?" I said while pointing my finger at the four of them. "The way Paul is handling his children, that is a quality I want in my future partner!" That quality was very attractive to me. In that instant I knew. I wanted my future children to have a father with those loving attributes. Paul's way of being with his children, the space of love he provided for them, his respect, that quality of his essence, was what I was pointing at.

As we passed Paul and the children, I pleasantly acknowledged and greeted all four.

Eliane and I continued our walk and repeated our upcoming schedule. What a great start to the day! I felt relaxed and happy. "Life is amazing," I thought!

11.2. Dancing Around the Galaxy

I woke up as the sun's rays peeked through the window and touched my face. I wasn't sure where I was. I opened my eyes and realized I was not in Belgium but on the other side of the world. Good morning, Breitenbush, I smiled! Another day in paradise was upon me. I wondered what adventures they had in store for us that day.

After a yummy breakfast, we all gathered in the Forest Shelter. Joost, Els, Marilyn, and Frank, the teachers in our retreat, explained the exercises. Honoring the Divine Feminine and the Divine Masculine was on the agenda for the day. I wondered what that meant and where it would take us. They explained that we all have a feminine and masculine aspect inside ourselves. Recognizing and understanding those qualities inside ourselves and each other was a powerful way to create inner balance and balance in our relationships.

Figure 29 Cabins at Breitenbush

In our exercises, the women would represent the feminine part, and the men would represent the masculine part.

We did the two exercises in two different times of the day. In the morning, the divine feminine was honoring the divine masculine. Men were laying down on the floor, heads together in the middle of the room, feet towards the wall. The women, representing the divine feminine, were invited to honor the men as the embodiment of the divine masculine with our dance and song. We drummed and danced and sang in a circle around the men. What a wonderful and powerful experience - something I had never done before. I had never honored the men in such a beautiful, profound, and touching way. The men listened to the feminine voices and opened their hearts to receive those feminine energies and love. It was powerful to open my heart and love and intentionally honor the men. I noticed the men were opening their hearts and willing to receive this precious gift. I was eager for the afternoon, where we would take turns, and the men would honor and bless us with their song and dance and drumming.

Paul: I did not participate in honoring the divine masculine exercise in the morning. My assignment was to be with and care for the children while they were playing outdoor games. We were in the woods and meadows and constantly on an adventure.

For many years, I explored what it meant to be a man in this world. I was born into a culture that had cast the male role as a soldier in war and then husband, provider, loving partner, and teacher in times of peace. These roles tended to bleed into each other in day-to-day life and create internal turmoil and confusion, which created a complex quandary. How can I be a male with both masculine and feminine qualities?

My studies made me realize that there are two masculine and two feminine forms operating in humanity, especially in the West. One form is the old masculine, which is primarily about domination and control. And there is the divine masculine, which is compassionate, loving, and powerful in life and action. The old feminine operates through manipulation to achieve her goals, while the divine feminine manifests through truth and love to reach her goals. My search let me attend the Practical School of Wisdom and Compassion to learn with Frank Coppieters and Marilyn Powers.

In the afternoon on that day in Breitenbush, I was part of the male's gift to the women. We honored the divine feminine by dancing, drumming, and singing to the women as they lay in a circle on the floor. It felt great to provide this loving energy to our female classmates and our new Belgian female friends.

At the end of this hour-long ceremony, as was our custom, we mingled and shared heartfelt hugs and expressed words of gratitude and appreciation. It was at this point that a most profound event occurred.

I looked across the room through the grateful milling participants and saw Mieke standing, looking in my direction. In her eyes, I clearly saw a miniature galaxy and two people dancing around the edge of that galaxy. I had never seen anything like that before in anyone's eyes, and it really transfixed my attention! It was striking, and it touched me to the very depths of my being! I had no idea what it meant. Because I didn't know Mieke very well, I chose not to share it with her; after all, she was much younger, from a different country, and I knew very little about her. I didn't tell anyone and silently wondered what that could possibly mean.

I had given up on personal relationships at that time.

Mieke: It was our turn to lay down in a circle on the floor in the afternoon. I felt camaraderie and connection with the feminine energies of all women in the circle—what an impressive view and experience to observe all those men standing there around us. It was a little intimidating, to say the least. I felt their loving and respectful intent very deeply. I wasn't used to being approached like that. I wasn't sure how to receive this and open myself fully and take it all in.

I closed my eyes and tried to relax. Then the sound began. Masculine voices filled the air; they blended together accompanied by drums directly projected towards us. I heard the men moving around in a circle. Their voices and drumming increased. Occasionally, I opened my eyes and looked at the men who were sending their love and respect our way. I had never experienced such a powerful masculine vibration, a gift of honoring, directly and openly transmitted toward me. It was overwhelming in a very positive way. I was also aware that it required me to open my heart completely to receive the gift in its fullness.

We all got up and shared our experiences when we finished the exercise. I didn't know Paul well at that time. I had no idea that he was not there in the morning. I wasn't aware that he looked into my eyes and saw two people dancing around the galaxy, which touched him to the core of his being. Paul had not mentioned anything about that.

After the event, everyone parted for some free time before the next delicious Breitenbush dinner delight.

11.3. To Eat or Not to Eat

Our incredible time in Breitenbush was about to end. One part of me didn't want ever to leave this magical off-the-grid place hidden deep in the woods, while the other part of me knew there was many more adventures waiting for me. I was eager to get back on the road again and explore more of this beautiful and intriguing America.

We had finished our last morning gathering, and I was starving! That often happens when I do energy work. My body and energy field were processing so many things simultaneously, and I had worked up a huge appetite. It was hard to imagine that this would be my last Breitenbush meal. I had savored a delectable buffet-style meal three times a day, including vegan, vegetarian, and gluten-free options, and a beautiful salad bar, delicious entrees, and a variety of tasty herbal teas. Every meal was a full-flavored nurturing moment for me and an opportunity to connect with my new friends.

My stomach was growling loud! I was impatiently waiting for the dining hall to open. I wondered what they would serve for our last lunch. I peeked through the glass door to get a glimpse of the menu written on the board. Great! The second bell rang, and the door opened.

Full of expectation, I walked up to the very familiar and much-loved buffet. I grabbed a plate and a bowl for the soup. It all looked so delicious. Carefully I started filling up my plate to fit as much as possible onto it. I piled up one delicacy after the other, and I needed a second bowl for the delightful salad with homemade dressing. I wanted to relish it all. I planned to eat slowly, savor every little bite, and capture this experience forever in my memory!

With a growling stomach, my plate filled to the rim, and the two bowls within hand's reach, I looked around for a place to sit—most tables inside were filling up fast. In front of the room, I saw Paul and his children sitting at a large table. I walked up and asked if I could join them.

"Sure," Paul said, "please join us." I noticed he was patiently helping the children with their lunch. He cut their food and made sure they had water, napkins, and utensils before eating his food.

Hungry as a ravenous bear, I placed my plate and two bowls on the table. I served myself a cup of delicious tea, collected utensils and a napkin, and sat down.

I looked at the mountain of food in front of me, the delicious bowl of hot soup, and the colorful salad. I was delightfully considering what to eat first.

Then something extraordinary occurred.

I picked up my fork to delve into my steamed vegetables. I looked at the bright green broccoli as I brought it to my mouth. As I was about to eat it, something strange happened. I felt that my hunger had vanished. When I walked towards the table, I had felt this all-consuming hunger. After I sat down and was about to eat my first bite, the hunger was gone. I did not understand. For sure I will eat, I thought, resisting this feeling. I bit into the broccoli - my body emphatically opposed. It was bizarre. My voracious appetite had vanished entirely. I also knew I wasn't going to have a second bite!

Mystified at what just happened, I felt confused, frustrated, and disappointed that I couldn't eat this anticipated last Breitenbush meal.

Completely stymied, I had to throw away the massive plate of delicious food, the soup, and the salad. I couldn't believe what had just happened. I could only feel the reality of it.

After lunch, the group exchanged addresses, emails (those that had one in 1998), and phone numbers to keep in contact. Paul and I exchanged our information just as we did with everyone else. There was no clear indication at that time that Paul and I would connect at a later date.

We all said our goodbyes. Frank invited the whole group to gather one more time at his house for a drumming circle later in the week. After that, we Belgians would return to our lives in Belgium.

We hugged each other and said our goodbyes. The Americans were going back to their homes and lives. We Belgians stayed with our guest families for another week and were eager to do more exploring. We knew we would see each other one more time at Frank's home.

I had such a powerful time in Breitenbush. With lots of gratitude in my heart, I said my last goodbye to the Breitenbush River.

As promised, Tommy and Leslie arrived to collect Eliane and me and drove us back to Jane's home at the Willamette River in Portland.

So, what happened during my last lunch?

At the moment it happened, it didn't make any sense! It truly confused my rational mind. Now, looking back, I know what happened! By sitting down with Paul and the kids, I experienced a feeling of oneness. Being together lifted my sense of separation. I felt satisfied and complete when our souls were reunited. There was no need for anything; our union nurtured me in all ways. I felt complete. I wasn't hungry anymore; I felt energetically at peace on all levels of my being. Only my mind couldn't reach that level of knowledge.

11.4. Mount Hood is Calling

Figure 30 Mount Hood and Hood River Valley

Another week in Beautiful Oregon was awaiting us. I had traveled through the East Coast states of America as a 19-year-old. This trip was my first time on the West Coast. The natural beauty in Oregon was impressive, and majestic Mount Hood in the far distance caught our attention. We could strongly feel the mountain was calling us. Eliane, Dirk, and I (the three Belgians) followed our gut feeling and answered the mountain's call with a rental car. Mount Hood is an 11,235 feet (3,424.4 meters) dormant volcano with year-round snow close to Portland. We explored the mountain's summit and stayed at the 1936 - 1938 constructed Timberline Lodge on the south side of Mount Hood at a 6,000 feet (1,829 meters) elevation.

From our lodge room window, we watched the sunset and discovered a beautiful blue lake in the distance in front of us. We all agreed to go swimming there the next day.

While waking up the following day, I observed the big old historic wooden beams above the ledge of my bed. I wondered who else could have slept in that room since 1938 and watched these beams.

The morning sun peaked into our room and motivated us to get going. We packed our bags and went for a fantastic breakfast in the Cascade dining room.

It was a perfect swimming day. The sky was cobalt blue, and the air was pleasantly warm. Trillium Lake was situated 7.5 miles (12.1 km) South-Southwest of Mount Hood. To make sure our towels stayed dry, we left them on the sun-heated rocks next to the lake. Mount Hood was reflected beautifully onto the lake.

A refreshing swim in the chilled mountain lake water made us return quickly to our towels for some sunbathing. We witnessed the mighty forest of fir trees around us from our towels, enjoyed the warm sun on our skin, and had fun.

A little further away from us, I noticed a few people, who I assumed to be locals because they sounded American. Eliane, Dirk, and I talked about what to do next. I decided to approach the locals. I introduced myself and told them we were tourists who didn't know the area. I asked for their suggestions on where to go.

A great place to go is Hood River, one of them suggested. It is a beautiful town famous for its windsurfing and orchard valley. "How do we get there," I asked. The man instructed us to drive back to the main road, turn left, and follow the road until we got to Hood River. "It is not far at all," he explained. Following the instructions, we were off on our next adventure.

After 20 minutes of driving through the forest, passing no signs on the road, we all agreed that we were lost and not going the right way. This man had clearly stated that Hood River wasn't far. In European terms, not far is for sure less than a 20-minute drive!

In America, "not far" can be up to three hours or more! We didn't know. At that moment, we all agreed that we were lost and better turn around and go back. Then I said, "Let's give it one more minute." After precisely one minute of driving, there was a big sign on the road reading "Hood River, 35 miles". At least we knew we were not lost and were going the right way.

Hood River, located on the south shore of the Columbia River, divides the states of Washington and Oregon and is bordered by high hills and two large mountains - Mount Adams to the north in Washington and Mount Hood, which we just left, to the south in Oregon.

Figure 31 Mount Adams and Paul on bike. 2018

Finally, we arrived at the cozy little town with cute little shops and inviting restaurants. By now, we had grown a big appetite and agreed to have a nice lunch at the Hood River Hotel on the corner of Oak Street and First Street.

After entering the hotel's restaurant area, the waiter asked if we wanted a table inside or outside. "Outside, please," I immediately replied. I wasn't coming from Belgium to sit in an air-conditioned restaurant while the sun was shining, and the feeling of summer was in the air!

The waiter asked me to walk toward the front door and find a table on the outside terrace.

I led the way through the door and stepped out toward Oak Street. A car coming from the left passed the restaurant in front of me. The person driving the vehicle turns his head to the right, toward me and looks me straight in the eyes. Our eyes locked. Recognizing this person, I threw my arm up in the air. It was Paul Benton from the retreat. All this happened instantly and simultaneously, without thinking. My arm automatically went up the moment I recognized Paul. I started waving my hand and gave him signs to come over.

He parked his car and joined the three of us at our table in front of the hotel restaurant.

"What are you doing here?" I asked Paul. We followed our inner guidance on our travels, and I didn't expect to see anyone from our group while we were traveling around. Paul said: "I live here! I should ask you, "What are YOU doing here?"

"You live in Hood River, I asked?" "Yes," he said. I was on my way to pick up my children from daycare."

Let me ask Paul to share how he experienced this powerful and unexpected synchronicity in his own words.

65

Paul explained: I returned from work and headed towards daycare to pick up my children. I was taking an alternate route which I rarely do and was surprised and delighted to see some of the people from our retreat. I pulled over, parked, and joined them at their table. They related their experiences on Mount Hood and Trillium Lake and were wondering what other sites would be interesting. They were thrilled to see such mountains and rivers, for their homeland in Belgium was relatively flat.

Some of my favorite sights in the Columbia Gorge are the many waterfalls cascading from the nearly mile-high cliffs into the Columbia Gorge. That should impress them! I thought. I just happened to have a recreational map of the Gorge in my car. I went to the car to fetch it and pointed out several waterfalls that they would pass on their way to Portland. Two were unique and not often visited and only a short trail away from the Columbia Gorge Highway. It was a lot of fun to see the Belgians, and I would have loved to join them for lunch, but I needed to pick up my three children.

Mieke goes on: And on the road we went. Map in front of us, instructions handy, we headed west back to Portland. The Columbia Gorge was magnificent. The Columbia River cut a path through a mountain range to make its way to the Pacific Ocean. It is not a small mountain range, for the river is banked by basalt lava cliffs. Some of them are more than 2,000 feet high.

We had a great time discovering the magical waterfalls and enjoyed the pristine natural beauty of the forest, flowers, bushes, mosses, trails, almost like a fairyland. We found all the waterfalls Paul had mentioned and saw many more! Exhilarated and exhausted, we arrived back at Jane's house.

After a tasty meal, I enjoyed a long hot shower. I was still in the bathroom when the phone rang. It was Paul. Jane knocked at the bathroom door and handed me the phone. "It's Paul," she said,

"He wants to know how the rest of your journey went today." Paul and I talked on the phone for about two hours. I'm not sure what all we talked about. I remember that it was effortless, a lot of fun, and very satisfying.

Paul: I wanted to know if they had found all the waterfalls I had pointed out on the map. I was curious about their experience. After all, Multnomah Falls is the second-highest waterfall in the Continental US, with a 620 feet (200 meters) free fall.

The phone conversation with Mieke that started as an inquiry into their experience lasted over two hours! Since they had such a great time appreciating the waterfalls and the beautiful nature, I suggested that the four of us should go to Tamanawas Falls together.

Figure 32 Multnomah Falls. Elaine, Dirk, Mieke 1998

11.5. Tamanawas Falls

Paul: Tamanawas Falls on Mount Hood is the sacred location where the native American Elders did a ceremony to open the heart of the mountain in 1990.

Mieke, Eliane, Jane, and I met at the Tamanawas trail at the appointed time. My dog Beauregard was with me.

It takes about an hour to hike to the falls. The trail ambles upstream always within sight of the rushing stream, which tumbles over a series of tiny waterfalls. This scenery provides wonderful sounds and views along the way: Engelmann spruce, Western Red-Cedar, and Douglas Fir are forming the forest canopy. We reached the canyon through which the Cold Spring Creek cascades on our journey.

Mieke: On the trail, I sensed an energy between Paul and me. There was something there. I wasn't sure what it was or what to do with it.

Paul: As we were admiring nature in all its glory, for a brief moment, I thought I saw a native American couple walking up a trail on the other side of the canyon (there was no trail there at that time). By the time I mentioned it to Mieke, they had disappeared. Was this a sign or an illusion? I am still not sure.

Mieke: When I felt this energy between Paul and me, Paul mentioned that he saw two native Americans, a man and a woman walking on the trail on the other side of the river. He asked me if I could see this. I looked, not with my physical eyes, but I could see them in my mind's eye, which was an intriguing and unusual experience. Not understanding this, we just kept walking further in silence.

After walking for a while, we decided to take a break on a huge log lying by the river. Paul and I were sitting very close to each other. That was the first time we both felt the energy between us and decided to act on it by gently holding each other for the first time. Nothing made any sense, but we both felt this unusual energy pull between us.

Walking further through the forest, we arrived at a magnificent and impressive view of the Tamanawas Falls. We enjoyed the falls from the trail, but we decided to follow one of the paths down for a closer look. We noticed that some people were sitting in a shallow cave behind the falls and decided to pursue the climb. To reach the grotto behind the falls, we had to climb the talus to the right of the falls. Paul, Eliane, Beauregard (the dog), and I ascended the large rockslide with countless large boulders.

What was absolutely an eye-opener for me was how Paul trusted his dog to go with us! I was so scared seeing the dog with his four legs climbing those rocks! I always over-protected my dogs. I didn't think that would be something they could do. For me, this climb was a combination of focusing on my personal safety and letting go of the fear I was projecting onto the dog. An enormous lesson of letting go of control and trusting the dog! Beauregard did a fabulous job arriving with us behind the waterfall.

Nurtured by the energy of the falls, Paul and I enjoyed another very gentle romantic embrace! It was powerful and at the same time, very confusing! I had no idea what all this meant. Nothing made logical sense!

We had a captivating experience that afternoon and again, we said our goodbyes. We knew we would see each other one more time at the drumming circle at Frank and Kathy's house.

11.6. Paul's Dilemma - confiding with Jane - (Paul Speaks)

Paul: I had seen a galaxy in Mieke's eyes and two people dancing around the rim, and I had no way to hold the experience. I had given up on love and relationship with women.

I recently went through a devastating divorce and child custody battle with Paula and her heartless lawyer. I had won custody of the three children and was recovering - but my heart was still severely damaged. It had been slapped around and stomped on by a ruthless lawyer.

Christopher, the youngest, was not quite four years old. We were living in a house owned by my sister Cathy. I had sold my two homes and two lots to pay off all the debts that Paula and I had incurred. I had nothing left but a car and the responsibility of raising and caring for three wonderful young human beings!

I was starting over. I had several part-time jobs. I was a pre-surgical massage therapist at Mid Columbia Medical Center in The Dalles, where I also taught tai chi. I had my private massage therapy practice in an office I shared with another therapist. Financially, I was barely making ends meet. And now this. A chance encounter with a younger woman from Belgium.

Over the course of the next week, I would come to realize that, yes, I was on a journey of the heart. I was being guided or, more accurately, pushed, pulled, and prodded by unseen forces!

I confided with my friend and classmate, Jane Pauli, in the depths of my confusion. Jane had graciously hosted two Belgian participants in our retreat; Eliane and the mysterious Mieke!

I was in this quandary of what was happening to me. What was going on? Jane said, "It is pretty obvious to me, when I read your energies, I intuit that you are in love."

When she spoke that, I immediately recognized the truth of that. It was at the same time exciting and terrifying. I was falling in love with this woman I had just met and barely knew. The truth hit me like a ton of bricks. This was an impossible situation!

The feeling was intense, unexpected, wonderful, and yet mystifying. I was being guided to follow my heart and not listen to my shouting mind.

Now what......?

11.7. Drumming Circle

Mieke: Our Belgian/American group had consented to come together one more time for a drumming circle at Frank and Kathy's home in Portland. That day had arrived; it was July 31, 1998.

Three of the Belgians (Dirk, Eliane, and I) carpooled. We arrived at Florida Street and recognized Frank and Cathy's home. The sun pattern above the door was a unique giveaway. We parked right in front of the house, and the three of us walked up to the door.

Figure 33 Frank and Kathy's home in Portland

Paul and his three children had arrived at the exact moment and walked with us up to Frank's door. We pleasantly exchanged greetings, and one of the kids rang the doorbell.

Kathy opened the door. Surprisingly, her face was white and she didn't look very healthy. With a questioning look on her face, she saw the seven of us standing in front of her and exclaimed, "What are you doing here?" Puzzled, we looked at each other and reminded her, we were there for the drumming circle!

"What?" she said. "I am sure that I called everyone to let them know I canceled the event. I am very sick and decided we can't do the drumming circle." We looked at each other again in amazement. None of us knew about the cancellation.

Paul and I explained that we didn't receive her message, and Kathy reiterated she let everyone know! Paul, his children and we (the three Belgians) didn't get the message for whatever reason. But there we were, gathered together at the door.

Obviously, the drumming circle wasn't happening. What now?

Paul asked if we were hungry and suggested going out for dinner now that we were all gathered there anyway. What a great idea! We were all in.

Dirk, Eliane, and I stayed briefly at Frank and Kathy's home while Paul brought his children to his ex-wife. The four of us were ready for our next adventure. Paul asked if we liked seafood and suggested his favorite fish restaurant at the Willamette River waterfront in Portland.

What a fantastic evening. I felt so good! Another exploration night in Portland. I so enjoyed the waterfront views and the many choices on the excellent seafood menu. This is what freedom tastes like!

This was my second trip to America; I felt so much gratitude for all the magnificent experiences that came my way. The unexpected adventures and synchronicities continued.

Excellent dinner! Paul and I were sitting across from each other at the table. Somehow Dirk and Eliane got into a conversation with each other, and Paul and I shared about our life situations. I shared that I was living by myself with my golden retriever, Rayca. Paul replied that he was living with his three children and his dog, Beauregard. We connected and talked about our work situations, differences in culture, families, and many subjects we were interested in. We delved into alternative healing modalities and the topic of consciousness. We seemed to be interested in similar subjects. Paul described the cranial-sacral therapy that he was studying. "There is a circulatory system of cerebral spinal fluid in the head and spinal cord that is vital to life. No cranial-sacral rhythm, no life!" he explained.

Our conversation was spontaneous, effortless, easy, and fun. We had a delightful time. I wasn't thinking ahead; I was in the moment, being very present and enjoying our experience. The synchronicities that had unexpectedly brought us together repeatedly had caught my attention. I wondered what that was all about. But no thought entered my mind that there could have been more to the story between us.

Paul: We were enjoying each other's company a great deal, and it seemed that synchronicities were putting us in the same place at the same time. It was a bizarre situation. We were very different in so many ways and yet seemed to relate very effortlessly, and it caused me start wondering if there was something more there.

11.8. Quest for Understanding!

Mieke: Why all this synchronicity, I wondered? Why were Paul and I brought together repeatedly in these most unexpected ways? I wanted to know what this was all about. Nothing made sense. I thought there must be an explanation, and I wanted to figure it out.

I knew Paul had one more afternoon off work before the Belgians flew home. I had an idea. I called Paul and suggested I would come to Hood River and spend that afternoon with him, hoping we would find more answers to what was really going on here and why we experienced all of the synchronous events.

That same evening there was also an event in Portland where Peruvian Native Elders would speak about the well-known 2012 prophecies. Many people from our American/Belgian group had heard about this event and decided to go to that talk, Paul included.

I thought this would work out perfectly. I would go to Hood River, spend the afternoon with Paul, and in the evening, we could drive together to the Peruvian Elder-talk in Portland.

Paul agreed that was a great idea. He was working in The Dalles Hospital that morning, and I suggested taking the bus from Portland to Hood River. By the time he was back from work, I would meet up with him in Hood River.

"That sounds great," Paul replied, "except there is one problem. There is no bus between Portland and Hood River." "What?" I respond, dumbfounded. No bus, how is that possible? Living in Belgium, buses are going everywhere you want to go. How could there not be a bus from Portland to Hood River? I was shaking my head, not understanding the situation. I thought for a moment looking for another solution.

"Alright, then I will take the train," I said. "There is no train either," Paul responded. Now I was completely confused. "What do you mean there is no train," I asked, crunching my eyebrows, trying to figure out what he was conveying. "There is for sure no train from Portland to Hood River. There was one in the past before Amtrak", he said. "The railroad system changed, and they eliminated the passenger trains in the American West." "What?" I asked. In Belgium, our train system is everywhere. You can take a train (depending on the time of the day) every 10 to 20 minutes in any direction you want to go," I replied in disbelief. "Nope," Paul replied. "No train either."

There was a silence. I was not able to comprehend the truth about this. Paul responded breaking the silence. "Let me check something," he said. Paul went to check the phone book. "Yes, it looks like there is one Greyhound bus traveling from Portland to Hood River that day. But you have to reserve your seat in advance. The Greyhound buses are the only option for inter-city travel, and the schedule is minimal. Sometimes there is only one bus a week," he stated.

"Ok, well, then I will take that bus," I said still shaking my head, stunned. How can that be possible that there are no buses or trains from such a big city as Portland to Hood River, which is only one hour away, I wondered. And you have to buy tickets in advance? I could not comprehend! At least we found a solution!

We had a plan, and the day arrived. Jane dropped me off at the Greyhound bus station in Portland.

As Paul had suggested, I took a seat on the left side of the bus, where I had the best view of the beautiful scenery of the Columbia River. Breathtaking! I relaxed into my seat admiring the powerful scenery presented before me. I was still unable to comprehend why there would be no buses and trains available. I couldn't figure that one out. It didn't make any sense to me.

I was amazed by the magnitude of the Columbia River. I had never seen a large river like this with a background of massive rock formations.

Figure 34 Columbia River Gorge

As I relaxed into my seat, I wondered what was to come next. In my mind, I summed up everything that happened so far; all the synchronicity that brought me to the decision to take a bus to Hood River in the hope we could unravel this mystery.

I let all the strange occurrences re-appear before my mind's eye, one by one.

- Before I sat down for my last lunch at Breitenbush, I was starving and could hardly wait to savor the meal. At the moment I sat down at the table with Paul and the kids, I couldn't eat one bite! Which made me mad and confused. I was very disappointed and couldn't understand what was happening.

- When I noticed Paul's dedication, quality of love, patience, and respect toward his kids, I pointed it out to Eliane. At that moment I was convinced I wanted those qualities in my future partner.

- Listening to the call of Mount Hood and following our guidance and suggestions of other people, we ended up in Hood River. When I stepped outside the restaurant to choose a table, Paul was driving by, turning his head towards me while driving, and we looked straight into the eyes of each other. Automatically my arm went up in the air.

- We didn't receive the cancellation notice and showed up at the drumming circle. Kathy was convinced she had reached everyone about the cancellation.

- A young native American couple appeared in our vision while we walked next to each other on the trail to the Tamanawas Falls. We both saw the same scene in our inner vision.

- The effortless hours of easy phone conversations with Paul after returning from the Falls. In that conversation, we both openly recognized and acknowledged the unusual synchronicity. After noticing these unexpected occurrences, Paul revealed his first profound experience in Breitenbush where he saw a Galaxy in my eyes with two people dancing around the edges. He hadn't dared to bring that up until this point.

Now we both openly questioned the situation. Noticeably, messages were coming our way. Some force was trying to tell us something. Honestly, I didn't have a clue why this was happening.

I didn't know that Paul's experience was more substantial regarding his feelings toward me. For me I was sensing things between us, but I couldn't place any of them. It didn't make sense and acting on the feelings physically felt awkward to me. The purpose of my trip was to connect deeper within myself. I was not open or even looking for a new relationship. Paul and I lived in two different cultures, and we were from two different generations with a 21-year difference between us. Nothing made sense.

I wanted to know why all of this was happening. That afternoon with Paul was powerful and intense and brought more confusion. I felt at ease in Paul's presence. I relaxed deeper into myself. But then fear arose in my mind when we attempted to come closer on a physical level. I was not able to relax and surrender to his embrace. Besides that, fear, the afternoon was amazing and enjoyable. We explored Hood River and each other, but still we had no clue what this was all about.

We had one more event together before I left for Belgium - The Peruvian Elders Prophecy event. We hopped in the car ready to drive to Portland, curious what the predicted 2012 prophecies were all about.

Notes from Paul's Diary:

On Monday, August 3, 1998, I went to Jane's house (where Elaine and Mieke were staying in America) to do a cranio-sacral session with Mieke.

In the kitchen, we connected again very deeply, physically, standing by the refrigerator. The Wes Burden CD was playing. We were gazing into each other's eyes only for brief moments at a time! In tears, mostly tears of great joy, but in some moments, huge fear would show up. Breathe, Cry, Emote, Breathe, WOW!

I gave Mieke a cranio-sacral session and noticed Mieke was stuck in the first three chakras.

Additionally, my last meeting with the Practical School of Wisdom and Compassion was that night. I rode with Jane to the class at Frank's and we talked. Jane saw a great love between Mieke and me. We spoke of this and wondered where spirit was leading us. She was so happy for us to have even touched such a great space.

Thursday, August 6 was our last meeting in person. Mieke came to Hood River on the bus so that we could be together. We met again - the eye thing. We chose to have lunch at the riverfront restaurant.

Then we went for a walk, watching the windsurfers, holding each other on the beach, having sand blow on us. Mieke withdrew when the feelings were too overwhelming. We walked and talked some more. Then I took her to my house. We touched and kissed and talked and lay together naked in the living room. We would have made love, but I couldn't! Was I not ready or too fearful? God only knows. It was the most beautiful connection I have ever experienced. I must follow spirits' lead with my heart to stay on this path. We played music, a tape I named "To Starshower from Sound of the Divine," the names we received in our Breitenbush retreat. I made this tape for her with my favorite music. The tape played one song at a time - it was magic and very scary all at the same time.

11.9. Oneness Experience

Mieke: It was my last day in America before my return to Belgium. In a quest for more answers, I had taken the bus to Hood River to spend the afternoon with Paul. There was great comfort in our time together, and still nothing made sense—the unknown triggered uncertainty in me, which brought up more questions than answers. We still had the Peruvian 2012 Prophecy event that night in Portland. Our time together wasn't over yet.

I hopped in the passenger seat of Paul's Red Ford Explorer, ready for our trip to Portland. I enjoyed sitting in that car. I was sitting much higher than in my Suzuki convertible I had just bought in Belgium. This vehicle gave me a much better view of the road and surrounding area.

Driving away from Paul's home, I said my goodbyes to Hood River. I assumed I would never return there again. I felt so much gratitude for the many places, people, and experiences that had come my way.

Driving through the heights and down the steep streets towards downtown Hood River, I admired the incredible view of the Columbia River in front of us. I recognized the many colorful kites of the windsurfers on the water I had observed up close that afternoon at the waterfront. What a view!

What happened next would become one of the most profound experiences in my life.

We traveled through the Columbia Gorge on Interstate 84; sixty miles of freeway that parallels the Columbia River. While listening to the CD, "Medicine Woman," I found myself in a profound state of deep peace. I felt deeply connected with Paul. A oneness-feeling with the Columbia River, with the music, and myself. I felt no separation between us and the environment around us. Everything blended into one deep sense of togetherness and peace. This profound oneness that I experienced reached far beyond my normal senses. I was not thinking - just being. A heartfelt oneness with all that is; a communion of self with all creation around me. During that magical hour, I felt the most peaceful and expanded I had ever felt. It happened spontaneously and unexpectedly. It also didn't feel extraordinary. It felt very natural and effortless, and I didn't realize what happened until I looked back at it afterward.

I experienced my authentic nature and the true nature of reality.

We arrived in Portland at the gathering and reconnected with many of our friends from the Breitenbush retreat. The event was about to start. Two Peruvian elders walked onto the stage. Their purpose was to share the ancient prophecies that came down through their lineage. The prophecies were about the year 2012. It was 1998, and the elders felt guided to share their sacred knowledge openly with the rest of the world. They expressed that it was time for everyone to become aware of the upcoming changes.

The Peruvian Elders began: *Something is about to change. Various ancient prophecies predict that change is coming to humanity. They further explained. This hope is a certainty. We are at the beginning of a new era. We all have a lot of responsibility. I personally believe and feel that the predictions of the Mayans of 2012 are of great importance. We believe that people's consciousness is going to change and expand. We hope that humanity will soon be able to unlock the mystery of what* *seems to be an increasingly frequent presence and encounters with those from other star systems.*

Mieke: Paul and I were sitting next to each other and were holding hands. We were like two teenagers, totally present in the moment. Paul and I were listening to what the indigenous elders were sharing, and at the same time we were aware of our connection and our last moments together. The message transmitted by the Peruvian elders touched us profoundly, and we truly enjoyed our final evening together.

We didn't think ahead. We weren't thinking about the future. We knew that this was the last evening, and the following day we Belgians were flying back home.

It was time now for Paul to drop me off at Jane's house. He first said goodbye to Eliane and Jane, who then went into the house and left Paul and me by ourselves outside for our last goodbye. We hugged each other and thanked each other for the very powerful times together. We knew many powerful synchronicities had happened, but we had no idea what to do with it or where it was leading us. Paul is two decades older than me; nothing made sense.

We had each other's email and phone numbers and at that moment decided to stay in contact. However, my life was in Belgium. Paul was living in Oregon and raising his three beautiful children and his dog Beauregard. Besides all those synchronicities, nothing made sense. And that is where we left it.

Paul: Nothing made sense!

11.10. Return to My Life in Belgium

Mieke: As I leaned back into my seat, the plane's speed rapidly increased. I was about to leave the American ground for the second time in my life. Bye bye beloved America! My experiences had again been incredibly powerful and fun.

We flew into Chicago where we had to wait a few hours for our next flight to Brussels. I was totally in my power. I felt so good about the powerful experiences I encountered, the majestic natural beauty I connected with, and the new connections I had made. I sensed inner peace, contentment, and an openness within myself.

Passing a telephone booth in the Chicago airport and now knowing how to operate one, I decided to call Paul and let him know we made it to Chicago.

I had some American coins left, which I couldn't return in the Belgian banks anyway. It felt so easy to connect with Paul, and I truly appreciated his friendship and the ease with which we could communicate. Again, we said goodbye, and that was it—no intent for more than a great friendship. Back in Belgium, we would keep in contact by phone.

I was about to return to Belgium, my home, my family and friends, the classes I was following in Centrum Gea, and my work as a counselor with disabled adults.

No boyfriend to return to this time. Even if being on my own didn't always feel comfortable, I was thankful for the space I had created in my life without an intimate relationship. But now, I was left with some confusion. Those powerful occurrences between Paul and I had caught my attention. I had felt a love and connection I had never experienced before, but none of our circumstances had made any logical sense.

The greatest joy in returning home was reuniting with my beautiful Golden Retriever, Rayca. If one thing had pulled my thoughts towards Belgium, it was my beloved dog. I knew he was in the best hands with my mom and dad in Deinze. He was the only thing I missed, and I wondered if he missed me as well. I knew our reunion would make us both very happy.

Rayca was over the top excited, and so was I. He jumped up and down, and his tail kept wagging for a very long time. We hugged and kissed each other with our hearts wide open. Feeling his soft long golden fur touching my skin gave me warm fuzzy feelings.

My mom was sitting at the table as I walked into the kitchen, and she asked how my trip was. I wanted to share openly and honestly what had happened but wasn't sure how to start this conversation. We were not used to expressing our emotions and sharing our personal inner experiences in our family. I never had open discussions with my mom on how I felt and what was going on inside of me. Emotions were mostly repressed and not openly shared. I went to my dad if I felt overly emotional and didn't know where to turn or what to do. He had the gift to hold the space and let me express fully before responding with his own feelings or thoughts.

I didn't know exactly how to respond to my mom's question about how my trip was. It had been extraordinary and fun. But how do I share about those synchronicities that had happened between Paul and me? I had no idea how to give them meaning in my own life, let alone trying to express what had happened to my mom. I quickly considered how to respond or what parts of the trip I would bring to the table.

When I heard her question, I felt a certain sadness and confusion. I was sad to have left America and the powerful times I had there, and there was confusion knowing I had to let it all go and move on with my life in Belgium. I didn't know how to integrate it all into the context of my life.

I decided to be open and share my feelings with my mom. Feeling vulnerable, I said, "I met someone there. His name is Paul, and he has three children. We had a great connection, but I do not know what to do with it."

My mom smiled and responded, "Well, you know, you cannot always get what you want in life." I know she meant it well, and I know there is truth to what she said. But it didn't solve my confusion.

It felt good that I could speak my truth to her, and I think my mom felt good that I trusted her to express my feelings with her. She didn't ask for any further information.

For the second time in my life, my return to Belgium created a strong contrast. Again, it felt strange to be back in Belgium. In America, I could openly express myself, be my true self, and connect on a heart level with almost everyone I encountered. There I experienced the profound inner freedom I so longed for.

It was time to let it go and move on with my life. I knew time would tell and bring me more answers. Trust the unfolding, I whispered to myself.

11.11. Leaving My Job

I did miss America, but I realized why I lived in Belgium and what I could learn from my experiences. I decided to focus on the present moment and integrate all the experiences and lessons learned.

I worked as a counselor in Home "Ter Linde," a residential facility for adults with a mental and or physical disability, for several years. I loved my work, especially the connections with everyone involved: the disabled residents, co-counselors, social workers, parents, family members, and the community.

I love to help people and enjoy human interactions. I believe I learn from everyone I encounter. Seeing people for who they truly are, powerful divine souls in a body having a human experience, no matter what physical, mental, or emotional disability they experienced in this lifetime, is what I truly liked about my job!

Unfortunately, my return to work was not a pleasant experience. Something in me had changed. I wasn't the same person I was before my trip to the USA.

And there was something else that I had noticed since I started working there that absolutely bothered me.

The extensive use of pharmaceuticals given to the residents didn't sit well with me. Most residents were given large doses of medications four times a day (breakfast, lunch, dinner, bedtime) carefully prepared in a weekly pill container. The residents were well trained to take their pills with a glass of water before each meal.

Regularly we had a group meeting with the counselors, the psychologist, and others who worked with the residents. I noticed a pattern after a while. Four times a day, we gave every person their daily medication. Some of them took a few pills, some of them took a lot of drugs. In the meetings, we discussed last week's behavior patterns of the residents, and then the psychologists decided, based on the stories being shared, how to adjust the medication.

In my opinion, many of the challenging behaviors of the residents are the result of the medications given. The drug is the true source of the undesired behavior, which is not recognized. The medication was adjusted until another undesired behavior pattern showed itself. And there we went again. We are adjusting medication, change in behavior, etc. A never-ending cycle and a substantial profitable income for the gigantic pharmaceutical corporations.

I saw through that game very early on and didn't like it. I noticed that 'big pharma' intended to guarantee an expanding income source and control the population. It is neither healing, supportive, nor respectful for the human being. Giving every meal a handful of medication to every single resident of the facility felt sickening and very disrespectful. When I questioned my colleagues about this, they seemed ok with it. They just obeyed because they were getting paid for it; it was their job.

A fortune is made by big pharma at the expense of the health and consciousness of the people. A travesty, in my opinion, that I wasn't willing to support any longer.

The first three months after my return from America were very challenging. Inner changes were taking place; my inner landscape was shifting. Fears and insecurities were popping up. I had so many questions. Who am I, what is my purpose, my true calling, what is going on with me? I longed for a soul partner by my side and a job to fulfill my higher purpose.

A feeling of disempowerment in my work situation increased significantly. Instead of spontaneously just being myself, I was trying to fulfill my colleagues' expectations. But inside, my fears and limiting beliefs prevented me from being who I wanted to be. Focusing on my fears only strengthened them.

I felt overwhelmed. Every day I was losing my alignment with myself and my integrity. I lost my motivation and inspiration, as they call it in the field, I was burned out. I needed to respect myself and make a change.

"What change do I make?" I asked myself. "And how do I go about this?" I just had taken on a loan in the bank to buy my first new car and added a little onto that loan to go to the retreat in America. "I can't quit my job; I need the money to pay my bills," I reasoned with myself. What to do? If I stay at the job, I will attract more negative situations until I listen and act on my intuition and inner knowing that staying there is not aligned with my integrity. If I quit, I will not have the money to pay my bills.

I decided to be open and honest and tell the truth. Without saying anything to my immediate collages, I called the head of the department in the institution, Tine. She was the person who could make the decisions. I told her I would like to talk to her and asked for a personal meeting. She was known for not being the easiest person to approach.

What do I have to lose? If I don't say anything, nobody can support me in finding a solution, I thought to myself. I decided to put all my cards openly on the table and tell Tine what was going on with me.

At the appointed day and time, I knocked at Tine's door. Even this was not a standard way of going about things; I felt calm and secure. I felt good about my decision. She opened the door and guided me to a chair. As I sat down at the table, she said, "tell me, what is going on?" "Why did you want to talk to me?"

Calmly, I explained that I felt burned out and needed to take care of myself. Removing myself from the job seemed to be the best solution. I shared that I wanted to get back into alignment with myself and figure out what I needed to do next. I also told her that if I quit my job, I would not be able to pay my bills, so quitting was not an option for me.

"So, what can I do for you," she asked? Forthrightly, I asked if she could give me the paperwork that would allow me to get unemployment. (Normally, you cannot go on unemployment if you quit your job on your own. If the company has a reason to let you go, they can give you the papers to go on unemployment.)

I did it. I was done talking. I had spoken my truth and asked for what I wanted. I presented a solution that would solve my challenge and gave me the space and time to figure out what to do next.

A silence filled up the room now. I had spoken my truth with ease. Tine had listened intently and had not interrupted me. She looked at me, and we both sat there together in silence.

It was in her hands now. If she said no, I would stay at the job until I found another job. If she said yes, that would solve my problem. I knew it would be a yes or no.

I wholeheartedly surrendered in that moment of silence. I had done my part. What lay ahead was up to the universe. Either way, I would be ok with her decision.

Then she broke the silence. "Ok," she said," I will do that for you. I will give you the papers so you can request unemployment. I appreciate your honesty and do not spread this story out everywhere. Please keep it for yourself". "Ok", I smiled. I felt a deep gratitude and appreciation for her in my heart because she had listened to her heart. She, too, used her intuition and acted with gratitude for me, I felt, because I had the courage to be open and honest. A deep sense of relief engulfed me! She handed me the paperwork for unemployment and had me fill out the form for putting in my two-week notice.

When I knocked at that door, I had no idea that I would leave that room with unemployment papers in my hand and a two-week notice approval to leave my job.

My life had just taken on a whole new direction, and I liked it! What a relief! I could see that Tine felt good about her decision as well. I walked away with a feeling of freedom and joy! My steps were light and bouncy!

I learned a huge lesson! If I am clearly expressing what I want, it can be given to me. It is harder to achieve when I am confused or not sure of what I want.

"Wonder what's next?" I thought to myself.

I had no idea what was to come next. I felt a huge relief that I had acted on my truth. Feeling free and joyful, I trusted my life's unfolding.

My last day at work was January 15, 1999.

11.12. Turning Point

Leaving my job had given me a welcomed break from the rat race. My inner compass had let me know it was time to move away from that which was no longer serving me. What was next? I wasn't thinking about next. I was listening to the signals of the moment and took steps towards what felt better.

Three of those significant steps all collided in that same month of January 1999. It wasn't consciously planned that way. A Darshan visit to Mother Meera in Germany, my first reiki initiation with Bernadette Van de Maele, and my last day at work -these three major events all stirred me deeply. It happened very fast. They brought with them deep feelings and inner shifts. I can easily say that since the Breitenbush retreat in America and my return to Belgium, my life had been an intense roller-coaster ride with unexpected ups and downs, in which my mind, emotions, and body were tested. Many times in those last five months, I had felt ill and experienced a lot of discomfort. My body responded to the many inner and outer shifts I was making. It was hard to keep up with it all.

I thought I should be delighted because I was free from the rat race. I could pay my bills, and I had the space to think about what I would like to do next creatively. Instead, I found myself spending a lot of time on the couch. My body was not able to do anything. My mind felt dull and uninspired. Even walking my dog or making food for myself and eating felt like an arduous task.

"What is going on with me? It doesn't make sense!" I thought to myself. Every day that passed, I felt less able to move. At a certain point, it felt like I was dying. A feeling that I have a hard time describing even to this day. Something major was going on, and I did not know what it was. The feeling of dying intensified as the days moved on. I needed some help!

Going to a mainstream doctor was out. I knew their approach; I have watched this happen many times. They would give me general prognoses, a prescription for a popular and sponsored pill, and some time off. I didn't need the time off. And I was not interested in any drugs. That would not address or cure the real cause of my symptoms. It would only serve as a band-aid on top of the wound.

I wanted to consult with someone willing and knowledgeable to look deeper into the true energetic causes of what was going on with me. I had studied and practiced many of these techniques myself in Centrum Gea. Unfortunately, I was not able to make a diagnosis on myself.

An idea popped up in my head. I decided to call Els Van Hogenbemt, my teacher in Centrum Gea. She is a general physician, homeopath, energetic healer, and in my opinion, also a visionary. She was so good that anyone who wanted a session had to book many months in advance. I knew I could not wait that long. I needed help right now! I decided to call her and leave a message on her answer machine. I would explain how I felt and ask if she could refer me to one of her best students that could help me out.

I picked up the phone and called Els's practice. I was ready for the answering machine, but she picked up her phone, to my surprise. I was shocked. "Els, you are picking up your phone!" I spoke out loud, completely surprised. Then I continued, still startled, "Hi Els, this is Mieke De Clercq."

"Yes, Mieke, I pick up my phone when my intuition tells me to do so," she answered, laughing. Still surprised, I said, "Els," I have no idea what is going on with me. Something does not feel right. I feel like I am dying, a very weird feeling. I need help and do not want to go to a regular doctor. I don't want pills, and I do not need time off. I know you are booked for quite some time. Do you have a student that you could refer me to that could help me?"

Els listened and was quiet for a few seconds. I surrendered, waiting for her response. Then she spoke. "Come tomorrow on my lunch break Mieke; I must take care of this." Then we hung up.

What just happened? Was I dreaming?

And this was not the end of this miracle! My best friend, Veerle, who had booked a session with Els several months prior, had her session right after Els's lunch break, which meant that Veerle was able to drive me to our appointments. More Divine intervention at play.

We parked at Centrum Gea where Els lived and practiced on the appointment day. While Veerle waited in my car, I walked into Els's office. I felt totally out of it. I thanked Els for making this possible at such short notice.

"Please sit down, Mieke," Els said while pointing at a chair. Els sat down in a chair right in front of me. "Let's see what is going on with you." She closed her eyes and went inside herself. I also closed my eyes and took a deep breath, trying to relax, knowing now that I was in good hands. I completely surrendered in that moment.

After about 30 seconds, Els opened her eyes and asked, "Mieke, what was the best thing that ever happened to you?" I was surprised at the question, but I immediately knew the answer.

"Els, the best thing that ever happened to me was the oneness experience I encountered while riding for an hour with Paul from Hood River along the majestic Colombia River toward the Peruvian Elders presentation in Portland. I felt such an inner and outer peace, a total sensory connection with all that is. I was at one with Paul, the river, the music, and the natural environment that surrounded us, " I replied.

Els continued asking questions about Paul, which made me confused and irritated. I wasn't there to talk about Paul; I wanted her to focus on me. I was there because I felt like I was dying.

Els continued. "Mieke, what I see is, the reason you feel that you are dying is because your life in Belgium is at its end. Your life is done here. You are supposed to be with Paul and the kids in America.

I looked Els straight in the eye. Her words penetrated deep into my core. She had spoken the truth. In a matter of moments, my body was responding. The tightness and pressure were releasing themselves until all tension was gone. The truth spoken had literally set me free. I knew at that moment what I needed to do.

My heart acknowledged what Els had just revealed. I sat there feeling the truth working its way into my consciousness.

I nodded to Els while all the synchronistic events flashed again into my memory. The galaxy that Paul had seen in my eyes, the loving way I had seen Paul nurturing his kids on the trail played in my mind as well as my hunger vanishing when I joined Paul and the kids at the table and the vision of the native American young couple. Our glances met as I walked out of the restaurant when Paul drove by. We were the only ones meeting up for the canceled drumming circle. The profound oneness experience. Our identical "386" phone prefix.

Where nothing had made sense before this moment, the significance of all these synchronicities fell into place. That's why all those things happened between us, I thought to myself. I get it now.

"So," Els continued, "where is Paul now?" I looked at my watch. "It is now almost six o'clock in the morning where he lives, and his alarm clock will go off any moment." Paul knew that I felt like I was dying, and he was supporting me with reiki and checking in with me by phone. He also was aware of my appointment with Els.

Els continued, "Well, Mieke, call him." "Right now?" I responded in confusion. "Yes, right now," Els answered as she handed me her home phone. "Well, I do have a calling card," I said as I reached into my purse to grab it. Every cell in my body was vibrating with clarity and certainty. I knew I had to make this call, and I also knew I had to be succinct and to the point.

I dialed Paul's number. He picked up his phone, and with a sleepy but very loving voice, he said, "Good morning, this is Paul."

"Hi Paul, this is Mieke," I responded. "Hi Mieke, how are you feeling? How did the session with Els go?" he answered back. "Well, Paul," I responded calmly and to the point, "I am in the session with Else right now in her office. Els saw that the reason I felt like I was dying was because my life in Belgium is done, and that I am meant to be with you and the children in America. And when she said that I immediately felt my body responding and returning to balance." "Oh, that is great," Paul responded. "So, what are we going to do now," I asked?

Paul paused for a few seconds and then replied. "Well, spring break is coming up. What if you come over and be with us here in Hood River, and we will see how it goes. I will check with the children to see what they think about this. They must be included in the process." "Ok, that is a great idea," I replied. Then we concluded the call.

As I was hanging up the phone, Joost, Els's loving and supportive husband, came in the room with a plate of sandwiches for her lunch.

"Tell him," Els admonished. I looked at Els with a questioning look. "Really?" "Tell Joost what just happened and what you are going to do." Els knew that speaking it out loud to a third person and sharing it with the world was my next step. Now I had to act on it. Joost looked at me with inquiring eyes. I wasn't sure I would be able to get the words out. "Joost, it looks like I might be moving to America." It felt like I had just dropped a bomb. By speaking it aloud, I initiated the creation process. As said, "in the beginning was the word."

Speaking it aloud to Joost was the best thing I could have done at that moment. It prepared me to declare my newfound truth to my family and my friends.

Joost responded positively and was happy about it, which was also great support. I thanked Els again for being so generous with her time and helping me get to the core of the dis-ease I had felt. I had walked into her office like I was dying and walked out in an entirely transformed reality. Now I knew my direction and my purpose.

As I walked very slowly towards my car, Veerle came out and asked how my session had been. I felt quiet inside. My whole reality was in the process of changing. I looked at her and said, "Veerle, it was all-powerful. I need time to digest it all, so while you are in your session, I am going for a walk in nature. After your session, we both can share." I didn't want my information to distract Veerle from getting the most out of her long-awaited session.

I slowly walked in inner silence. My mind had seldom felt so quiet and at peace before. The large trees were witnessing my first steps into my new reality, into my new life, into a new beginning.

When Veerle returned, I suggested we go for a walk together to walk and share. I knew this was not going to be a quick share. I was also unsure how to share it because I was still assimilating and adjusting to the news myself. She agreed and I asked her to share about her session first. I wanted to give her my full attention.

The fact that I had to share this again in less than an hour, first to Joost and now to my best friend, Veerle, was a sacred gift. A practice in creation. I could safely share my truth with these two people I knew I could trust and be completely open with, which was crucial for me at this turning point in my life.

I asked Veerle not to share this information with anyone. Before sharing it with family and friends, I needed time to embrace my new reality first. I had no idea how long that would take. I needed time to incorporate it and allow my inner guidance to lead the way. Everything was about to change, and I didn't need anyone's input, questions, emotions, and thoughts. I needed all the space I could get to be with myself.

Driving home, I felt like a just popped-out butterfly not sure how to approach my new reality. In this session whit Els, I went through a metamorphosis: a rebirth, a transfiguration, a changeover. I knew soon it would be time to spread my wings and fly.

12. Vision Earth Changes - Gent, Belgium - Night of August 14, 1999.

Paul and I chose August 20, 1999, as our wedding day, considering the astrological aspects. No one in my family in Belgium had ever met Paul. Before starting my new life on the other side of the world, they at least needed to get to know him. We decided to get married in Belgium.

Figure 35 Mieke, Paul Rayca. Wedding Day

Figure 36 Jeroen, Mieke, Hugo, Anny, Paul and Leen

Figure 37 August 20, 1999. Deinze, Belgium

Figure 38 Mieke and Paul. Divine Intervention at Play

A stream of effortless synchronicities occurred from the moment we made that decision. Without request, friends and family offered solutions for everything needed to make this wedding an incredible event - from the wedding venue to the invitations, the menu, flowers, music, entertainment ideas, and even my wedding dress! All aspects of the wedding came spontaneously together, supported by friends and family. A co-creation at its best! The wedding became a joyful and relaxed event that people up to this day, 22 years later, are still talking about. Paul was loved and respected by all!

Carine, a Belgian participant at the Oregon retreat where Paul and I met, lived in Gent, where I was born. She offered us her home as a sacred place to stay while getting ready for our wedding. Carine took off for a week and left us her wonderful home to ourselves.

The walls in Carine's home, intentionally embedded with a crystalline structure, elevated the energy frequency in the house. The first night we were sleeping there, I received a powerful, life-changing vision in which I was a conscious participant.

In this vision, I was driving my car to Oostende, a coastal town in Belgium where I spent a part of my youth. There was snow on the side of the road, which indicated it was wintertime. I planned to visit my friend Nancy in England.

In real life, in 1999, Nancy was staying in England with her English fiancé, Phil. There was no underground tunnel yet to drive to England. The only way to cross the canal was by boat, which took about four hours.

I arrived in Oostende and went walking on the beach in my vision. Suddenly, I noticed little swirls in the sand in the corner of my eye. The sand was swirling down in little circles, as sand does in an hourglass. It caught my attention and I stopped to go look. In the distance, I saw a man also observing and investigating the swirling circles in the sand.

While observing this phenomenon, I realized that the circles were getting bigger and bigger. They opened up, and more sand was swirling down into what was becoming a larger crack in the Earth. The Earth was moving and very slowly opening up.

I cautiously looked in. I saw a deep hole with water and chunks of the Earth floating in the water. An open, deep gorge. It looked like a smaller version of the Grand Canyon. Seeing this shocked me, and I became aware that something serious was happening. Instantly, I realized that I needed to take immediate action. I was not sure how fast more shifts in the Earth would transpire.

I was not wearing shoes and decided I needed shoes and more clothes to handle what was about to come next. I quickly drove back inland to get the shoes and clothes at home.

By the time I arrived back at the beach, I had noticed that the cracks in the Earth had become more significant and realized the situation was becoming more serious. I knew that the Earth's crust was becoming weaker, and several crust parts were starting to move.

At that moment, I realized that England would be the first to go underwater and then the Belgian coast, of which the water would go inland.

I was not afraid but felt the intensity and impact of what was happening. I tuned deeper into the situation and knew I had to act as efficiently as possible. Going to England to visit Nancy was not going to happen. I knew that if the Earth started shaking, all kinds of things could happen. I felt the urge to inform others about what I saw.

As I walked into a building with about 30 people present, I noticed that nobody was aware of what was happening. I felt a responsibility to inform them.

Looking around, I questioned how I could get their attention. I noticed a pedestal in the middle of the room that I could use as a podium. I climbed onto it and called out, asking for everyone's attention.

I explained what I had observed in the sand and how I noticed the Earth was cracking open. I made them aware that the Earth was shifting and that many changes could occur. I shared the message I received about a re-birthing and shifting of the Earth, which was a natural occurrence in nature. It was important not to become fearful but to be aware of the situation at hand and act responsibly.

As I was explaining, suddenly the Earth started shaking violently. I informed the people that this was what I was talking about. It was direct proof of what I was speaking about.

As I spoke, the building turned upside down. Everyone was falling all over the place. I realized that I better let myself move with the shocks and then regain my balance in the process. While falling, I also realized that life could end any moment, that all could be over in a matter of seconds. It did not scare me. I felt very secure and experienced inner peace. I knew whatever would happen would be ok. A solid inner power inspired me to act swiftly and efficiently.

I did my best to speak calmly and suggested gathering their most valuable assets to the people living at the coast. I explained it would be wise to pack their car and move more inland until the Earth settled. We had no idea what would or could happen at that point. I made clear that it was of utmost importance that everyone stayed calm and did not panic. My words seemed to be influential.

After I spoke, I noticed three different responses in people.

One group of people profoundly thanked me for informing them. They knew this was precisely the guidance they needed. They would do what I suggested - pack up and move inland for the time being.

The second group of people thought I was completely nuts. They saw me as a doomsday-preaching nut case. They laughed and rolled their eyes. For sure, they would not consider any of what I had shared. They laughed it away and turned their backs.

The third group of people was attached to their homes and programmed lifestyles. Even if they believed me, they would not be able or willing to change their daily routines and habits. Their whole life was invested in that what they had built up. Packing up and leaving everything behind, even for a short period of time to secure themselves was not an option for them in their current mindset.

I understood all three responses. There was nothing wrong with any of them. Everyone had the free will to believe or do what they found best for themselves. I knew everyone had their unique soul journey and mission. I respected that.

After speaking my truth of what I saw was occurring, I felt the urgency growing to move on. There was no time to lose. Significant shifts could happen at any moment. In the building, I found blankets and gave them away to the people around me to keep themselves warm. In the end, I realized I forgot to keep one for myself. I knew I would be ok.

When I had informed everyone around me at the coastline, it was time for me to move inland and continue sharing with as many people as possible what was happening with Mother Earth; I got in my car and drove away.

At that moment, the vision stopped. My consciousness was starting to re-enter my present reality in Carine's home in Gent. Suddenly, I heard a voice abruptly saying, "WAIT!", "WAIT, we want to give you a date!"

Without resistance, I pulled my consciousness back again into the vision. I saw visually in large print the numbers 2008 written out in front of me, and at the same time, I perceived the numbers audible in sound.

Hearing the 2008 date created a great deal of confusion in my mind. I had never thought about the year 2008 before. On a global level, we were all intensely occupied with the year 2000 before its arrival. Because of the long-talked-about prophecies, the year 2012 was ingrained in my awareness and my DNA. 2008 came as a total surprise. It felt as if my DNA was being stretched open by receiving this new date in my awareness. It felt like friction in all cells of my being. A very interesting and weird feeling that is hard to put into words.

After I was given the date, again my consciousness was starting to re-enter my present reality in Carine's home in Gent. I became aware that I was in bed and that I just had received a stirring and powerful vision. Paul was lying down next to me, deeply asleep. I wanted to share with him what I had just encountered but knew that even if I woke him up, I would not have been able to transmit the intensity of the vision I had just experienced. I decided that the best way to go about it was to let Paul sleep, take a piece of paper, and write down what I had experienced and shown. I would tell him later in the morning when he was fully awake and aware.

Since that night in 1999, every detail and impression of that vision clearly stayed present in my memory. Many questions arose since. What does this mean? What will happen? Why did I receive this vision? For nine years (until 2009), I wondered what to do with this information.

When it felt appropriate, I shared my vision with open-minded people. I noticed that the message was often supportive for those I shared it with. Sometimes I had no idea why I felt guided to share with certain people.

Over time, I realized that this vision had shown me my task and mission: not to become fearful regardless of any circumstance and inspire others to do the same. 2008 came and went. Afterward,

I realized that a significant shift happened in 2008 on a financial and economic level worldwide. Also 2012 came and went. Many changes were happening then and are still happening now. We are shifting and changing as a people, as a global humanity; the Earth is shifting and changing in consciousness and awareness; even the cosmos as a whole is shifting and changing. The only constant is change and transformation.

I realized that if we weren't willing to embrace change and expand as humans in 1999, those more dramatic earth changes could have occurred in 2008. It was as if I saw the future from that frozen moment in time in 1999.

But we did change. We have been making many shifts in consciousness since 1999 and even more since 2008 and 2012. Look at us today in 2022! So many opportunities for expanding our awareness are available.

Humanity is waking up, one step at a time. For some of us, it seems like our collective awakening is a very slow-moving process, and not everyone is willing to change their habits and beliefs in a timely manner and for the highest good of all. Change is not always easy and comfortable. Sometimes it feels like a messy undertaking and an inner battle to me.

Then I frequently remind myself, "This is a free-will planet." We all learn our unique life lessons in our own time and space. The most important message is not to become fearful while we are shifting, changing, and waking up to a more benevolent reality on planet Earth and our righteous place in the cosmos.

13. Red Fire Ball in the Sky, Hood River, Oregon

Half a year earlier, I had made the big move from my life in Belgium to living in the USA. My life had changed drastically during those last six months. Besides leaving my European culture, friends, and family, I took on a new culture. I also married Paul, who is 21 years older than me and had full custody of his three small children. From being single in Europe, I had created an instant family in the USA in less than a year. The five of us were living together now in Hood River, Oregon.

I quickly realized that each culture has unique habits, beliefs, and norms. I was learning to adapt to a different reality than my homeland and, at the same time, adjust to married life with three children, talking about a fast-track experience at age 29! Overall, I made that jump very gracefully. But I also had very challenging moments.

Such a day was May 5, 2000.   I struggled inside – I struggled with myself and my adjustments to my new adopted reality. I felt heavy, negative, and ill at ease. I was facing my inner turmoil, and I knew that projecting those negative feelings onto Paul or the kids was not a fair thing to do. I didn't know what to do. I decided I needed some space and be by myself.

I told Paul I was struggling and would be sitting outside for a while. Right in front of the house was a huge ponderosa pine tree. I sat down on the ground with my back against the tree. Maybe that would support me getting grounded and re-balanced, I thought to myself.

At that time, we were renting Paul's sister Cathy's rental home on Orchard Road. In front of me was Cathy's horse barn. It was late afternoon and still daylight. As I sat there, feeling negative and wondering how to shake this feeling, I gazed above the horse barn.

Suddenly, I saw a bright red ball of light high in the sky, moving horizontally, coming from the left. From where I was sitting, the ball seemed to be the size of a small car. It turned with red moving fire flares like the sun's corona flares.

It was first moving horizontally and passed very fast in front of me. I detected no sound. Then with the same fast speed, it descended to the right sight of my vision. The fireball of light had landed somewhere in the distance behind the trees.

I was shocked! A deep sense of vulnerability arose inside of me. I was sitting there all by myself outside, and this red fireball of light had suddenly appeared and landed. My negativity and inner struggle had transformed now into a deep sense of fear. I had no idea what this was. I needed to get back into the house as fast as possible and explain what I just had witnessed to Paul. I didn't dare to move, but I had to run towards safety. I ran as fast as I could back into the house. Shaken, I explained to Paul what had happened.

I have no idea what that red fireball of light was to this day. I have seen UFOs and orbs, but this seemed to be something else. Maybe it was meant as a supportive message, a response to my inner cry for peace and balance. Who knows!

Paul: When Mieke was entering the house, she was visibly shaken. She explained to the best of her ability what had just transpired outside and that she felt vulnerable, frightened, and not sure what to do. I went outside to see if the red fireball of light was still visible. After searching the sky and seeing nothing, I came back into the house to reassure Mieke that all was OK. I did not doubt that she saw what she described. I had no reference other than the flying UFO I had seen by Mount Hood at age 18 in 1968.

14. Second Vision, on My Way to Bali

Before Paul and I met, he had previously done several workshops at the Human Awareness (HAI) Institute in San Francisco, created by Stan Dale. HAI holds a bold vision of a world where every human being is worthy of love, without exception, where we live a life enriched by self-acceptance, connection, and a deep sense of belonging to those we love. Paul and I married in 1999. We decided to participate in one of their experiential workshops, where we safely explored and immersed ourselves in the delicate terrain of love, intimacy, and sexuality. Those workshops were fantastic and powerfully freeing.

At the end of this weekend's workshop, the teachers informed us that Stan Dale organized a vacation trip to Bali, called "Bali HAI 2000", and any of the HAI workshop participants could join him. There would be no workshops; it would just be for the fun of traveling together.

Besides the few days in Paris after we married in Belgium, Paul and I decided this trip to Bali would be our official honeymoon.

Maggie and Peter, friends in Hood River, gracefully offered to take care of our children for those ten days. We booked our first exotic vacation with Singapore Airlines, the best airline company we ever experienced.

Something very interesting happened on the long flight from San Francisco to Bali. We were flying at night. Right before I drifted into sleep, I received a second vision in that in-between state.

In this vision, I was a man and an old shaman. I was living in a hut built out of clay and straw. The climate was tropical; I had barely any clothes on, and my old skin was brown and wrinkled. I had tied only a rag around my middle. My feet were bare. I was a wise elderly man, and people came to me with questions or needed help. I could communicate with the earth and the cosmos.

At that moment, I was in my hut with several people gathered around me. Known for reading tea leaves and smoke signals, people often came to observe and learn. I was used to having people around me while in mediation and doing rituals. As many times before, I was about to communicate with the earth and receive messages by reading smoke signals.

Slowly and in a meditative state, I gathered a hardened dried leaf that looked like a tiny wooden boat the size of my palm. In this leaf, I would soon burn some herbs as medicine. The herbs, smoke, and fire movement would bring forth the messages.

I welcomed the people around me as I moved deeper into meditation. While preparing the leaf with herbs and a few little twigs, I could feel the earth's energy. As we all united our energies together, I felt the message starting to come forth more strongly. I lit the herbs with some fire. The smoke began to form itself. Everyone around me was quiet and observed.

Immediately I noticed something unusual. The smoke presented was much stronger than I had ever experienced before. I didn't expect such a fast and robust reaction and immediately told the people around me to move further away from me. The earth was responding through the smoke in an intensity I had never seen before. I knew something was up. I could feel the earth's essence and her call to pay attention.

The hut filled with smoke in no time, and I ordered everyone to go outside. I told those around me that something was up! Something was going on with the earth, and she showed me it was serious and important.

The intensity of the smoke kept increasing. I centered myself deeper and opened my consciousness. I listened more intently to receive what the message was all about. I felt the earth was shifting and changing. Her intensity was increasing, and it was essential for us to know.

Then I felt my consciousness slowly coming back to where my body was located. First in my earthly body in the hut. Then I realized I was flying in a plane very high in the sky on my way to Bali. But before I got fully into my body in this time frame, they again showed me a date. This time it was the year 900.

It confused me a little. In 1999, in my first vision, I was given the date 2008, which was in my future. This time, in 2000, I was given the date 900, which was in my past—both visions were related to messages about earth changes.

This second vision left a profound impression on me. Had I tapped into another timeline, a past life? I knew it was me in that other time frame, and again I was a messenger—a messenger about the changes about to happen on earth.

15. GO HOME! - a Voice Commanded - Maui, Hawaii 2000

"Where do we want to live and create our new life together," Paul asked? I had just moved from Belgium to the USA and created an instant family. Paul, the three children, and our two big dogs were my new life now. A big task was in front of me - adjusting to a whole new lifestyle.

While living in Belgium, I had felt and followed my inner guidance and intuition. A powerful force of divine intervention had unexpectedly intervened. From two different cultures and two different generations, our lives gracefully merged. Paul, Andrew, Angela, Christopher, Beauregard (Paul's dog), Rayca (my Belgian golden retriever), and I were forming our new family. Seven souls united on a new adventure.

Where do we want to live? I had no idea.

As a 19-year-old, I explored the East Coast of America for three months in a student exchange program. I worked two months in a summer camp for disabled people in upstate New York and then had the opportunity to travel for a month with a group of international students. My travels took me from New York to Florida, which showed me a big part of the East Coast. When I married Paul in 1999, I moved to Hood River, Oregon, on America's West Coast. Hood River is a small and beautiful farming community between the mountains and the Columbia River. It is also famous for skiing, windsurfing, and hiking.

Hood River was the home for everyone in Paul's immediate family. And even more interesting, they all lived on the same street, Orchard Road. Paul's ancestors had settled there and started a fruit farm. To this day, his brothers are fruit farmers with pear and cherry orchards.

When I arrived in Hood River in 1999, Paul rented a small house from Paul's sister Cathy. He was working three different jobs to make ends meet. Now that we were together, we felt inspired to expand our horizons. We liked the idea of creating our domain in a different location that supports loving and active family life.

America is a huge country compared to Belgium. The state of Oregon is 8.2 times the size of Belgium. The population in Belgium is 11,626,500 and in Oregon 4,217,737. America provides a wide variety of climates and topography from seashores to high mountain ranges. "Where do we want to live?" we asked ourselves. How do we find our desired location?

Alternative healing had been the focus we were both pursuing even before we met. It was also the reason our lives had merged. Astrology was another subject we had both studied and consulted. We both were aware that every location on earth also had its unique astrological chart and energetic qualities and vibrations. Paul suggested we consult an Astro-cartographer to help us decide on a place for relocation. I had never heard about Astro-cartography. What a brilliant idea, I thought. I went online doing my due diligence. How does an Astro-cartographer work, and who is out there doing this? Julian Lee was the person we decided to contact.

We explained to Julian Lee that we were a family of five looking for a place to relocate. We also asked him some questions about himself and his work. Typically, Julian Lee consulted with a single person or a couple who desired to relocate. Bringing all our five astrology charts together to determine a location was not a frequently asked task.

We decided to book a consultation. Julian explained that in a first consultation, he would ask us to share more about ourselves, our lifestyle and occupations, what we were looking for, and what we were expecting from our future location. Then he would do the work of consulting our charts and the charts of different areas. In a final phone call, he would share what he had discovered and suggest a location based on the various charts.

I was eagerly awaiting that phone call. Soon, very soon, we could plan our new adventure, I thought. I was so curious to know where we would possibly be moving. When the phone rang, I was nervous and almost jumped out of my skin - only to be very disappointed to hear Julian asking us for more time. Bringing five charts together was not a standard request for him, and he needed more time. Julian presented a new date. I was not too fond of it that we had to wait a few weeks. I had to surrender.

Two weeks later, the phone rang at the appointed time. I impatiently sat down with pen and paper, ready to take notes full of anticipation. Julian mentioned that we would receive a recording afterward, but I still wanted to take notes during the call. We picked up the phone, and Julian's calm voice was put on speakerphone for both of us to hear.

"I am very sorry," Julian said, "I will have to decline your case. I will refund the $300 for my service. To stay in my integrity and live a peaceful life, I only want to share a possible relocation place when I am 100% sure and convinced that the research I did feels correct and accurate to me. I could not find a place to support all five of you in the way I would like. The closest I got to locations were Maui or Kauai, but I did not feel comfortable enough about suggesting these locations."

I was SO disappointed. So was Paul. Bummer! We got our $300 check returned to us in the next few days. We certainly appreciated his honesty and integrity.

Maui or Kauai? Hmm, interesting. Hawaii was the last of the 50th states to become part of the US in 1959. We had not considered moving there. We decided to look into it and do some research. The idea of moving to Hawaii became a seed planted into our awareness. What would it take to move there?

We decided to go for it and packed up all our belongings. We stored most of it in Hood River and only took those things we could get onto the plane with us. Our family of seven, the three children, Paul and I, and the two large dogs were up for a new adventure.

Figure 39 We moved to Maui, Hawai'i

Figure 40 Bananas in our garden

Figure 41 April 7, 2001. Paul's 52ⁿᵈ Birthday

Figure 42 Whale and Dolphin watching

Finding a place to live in Maui was quite an adventure! When synchronicities occur, my intuition tells me to pay attention! I did. It brought us to Alex and Jed, still dear friends to this day. They owned a beautiful Hawaiian-style home with a large garden with ocean views in Haiku. They lived on the upper floor of the house and were renting out the rooms downstairs.

The largest room was a studio with a separate bedroom, a bathroom, and a living room with an extra-large bed for the kids— a perfect fit for us. We were more comfortable than our first options the first few weeks of our life on Maui. By now, the kids were in school, and the dogs were out of quarantine. Living with Jed and Alex was a breath of fresh air. I started to ground myself more in my new Hawaiian lifestyle. With the help of another renter in the house, I quickly found a job as a cook in a natural foods store close by in Paia.

And then this happened.

One early morning, as I was coming out of my sleep and into the in-between asleep and awake state, I had a profound experience.

A clear and explicit voice made itself known inside of me. It was the most powerful masculine voice and vibration I had ever encountered. It spoke two words. Those were directed to me and deeply felt in the depths of my being.

"GO HOME," the voice commanded firmly. Those two words, "GO HOME," spoken with such a profound authority, depth, power, and intent, were felt in all the cells of my body.

I knew this was a personal message. I immediately opened my eyes and saw that I was in Jed and Alex's home in Maui. When I closed my eyes again, I went back into that in-between state where the communication had happened. That same voice shared more with me. The second communication happened more quietly and in the background. Unfortunately, by the time I came back into my full consciousness in the room, I couldn't recall the information of that dialogue. I knew my soul spoke the message.

GO HOME! Those words catapulted me instantly back into this dimension. Quickly I woke Paul up and told him. He was still half asleep. I took my pen and paper and wrote down what just had transpired.

Then my mind kicked in, and I pondered. I was clearly spoken to and told to GO HOME! I was living in Maui now. What was this instruction really about? Does this mean I have to go back to the mainland of America? Is that home? Does it mean I have to go back to Belgium, where I lived until age 29? It didn't feel like that was the home they were referring to. Where is home? A question I have been asking myself my whole life!

When I was 12 years old, I watched the movie ET. I recall the scene where ET was taking off in his spaceship, and I felt such deep sadness and envy. He is going home! I want to go home too! But where is home, I thought?

The words "GO HOME" and how it was commanded and expressed to me on Maui left a profound impact.

I realized that the words, GO HOME, were not pointing at a physical location on earth or anywhere else in the cosmos. The message was to feel home inside me - reconnect with my inner being, my inner self, my essence, my heart—that part of myself, connected to all that is, to the oneness of life.

This journey of coming home to my inner self, the love that I AM, has been the quest of my life. It's been my mind's battle, the struggle, the searching, the challenge.

I know now that I have always been HOME, inside myself. I even made a painting of it as a reminder. The painting reads, "STOP Searching. Remember the truth of who you are. Welcome home."

Going home is simple. But I find it is not easy. "Be still and know thyself" is another well-known verse that points to the way HOME.

Being still and going inside has never been easy for me. I constantly prefer to distract myself with outside influences and information. My heart knows better. Home is where the soul resides, in the silence of the heart. In this moment. Inside me.

After living one year on the island of Maui, it became apparent that we needed to move back to the mainland. In September, our oldest son would be going to middle school, and being a light-skinned, red-haired 11-year-old boy, people were telling us that he would not be treated nicely in Maui public middle school. Our children's well-being was our highest priority.

We left Maui and returned to Hood River, realizing that Maui was not our home to stay. However, Hood River did not fulfill that requirement either. Paul and I chose to journey together, hoping to find our perfect home location. We drove through California, Arizona, New Mexico, Utah, and Colorado. We ventured on a 5000-mile-trip to end up in Bend, Oregon, only 143 miles away from Hood River.

We made this decision because Bend was a healthy and safe place to raise the children, and it was close enough to visit Paul's parents and the Hood River family on holidays and other occasions. We wanted our children to know their relatives and stay connected.

We made the move from Maui to Bend in August 2001.

16. UFO in the Sky

Because I had been working in the natural foods store on Maui, I took on a position at a natural foods' bakery in Bend. Working in a bakery means early morning shifts. One early morning in 2002, I was driving to work in the old Lincoln car given by Paul's mom. I loved driving that car. It had huge windows with excellent visibility.

It was early morning before sunrise. I was driving on Cooley Road, about half a mile from our home and close to the Lava Ridge Elementary school and the Mountain View Middle school where our kids were going to school. Still tired but relaxed, I was looking straight in front of me, watching the road.

Suddenly, my head turned by itself 90 degrees to the left. It was not my intent. In that exact moment and in the direction my head had turned toward, I saw a clear metallic UFO high in the Sky. At that moment, I saw the UFO making a swift zigzag move which made it disappear in front of me as if it shot itself into acceleration and then disappeared. Immediately after I witnessed its maneuver, my head turned all by itself back to the front. I was able to see the road in front of me again. This whole event lasted maybe four seconds. It happened unexpectedly and spontaneously, without my conscious consent, like a synchronized movement between me and the spaceship. It seemed like I was supposed to see the UFO make a zigzag move and shoot into space.

After my head had spontaneously turned back facing forward, I said to myself out loud: "What was that all about?" I was obviously meant to see this. Some unconscious parts of me and the UFO were linked together. Telepathy? Synchronicity?

I am still wondering what that was all about. I do have my ideas. While my body was sleeping in my bed, my soul was on the ship. After waking up and driving to work, I sensed the UFO, and my soul wanted me to be aware of it. I was supposed to see the ship leave as a goodbye and see you later kind of a deal - a waving goodbye. It served as a reminder that I was there and that we were connected.

17. Black Circle in the Sky

It was 2004; two years after I had witnessed that UFO zigzagging and disappearing into space. Again, I was driving the old Lincoln car on Cooley Road. It was early morning, and I was on my way to work at the bakery.

In the same location where my head had turned to the left and I had seen a UFO, I noticed another unusual phenomenon. I was driving and looking in front of me. I saw a sizable pitch-black circle against the dark sky. What is that I wondered? A large balloon? It didn't seem to move, and it didn't seem to have dimensions. It felt like a flat black circle was hanging there in the sky.

I kept my eyes locked onto the black circle, which I thought could be a black balloon. When I passed the schools, the road turned to the right. The road would turn again to the left at the end of that road. I knew I would not be able to keep focusing on that black balloon as soon as the road turned to the right. Only when the road turned left again would I face the object.

After I turned right, I decided to drive faster and pinpoint in my mind precisely the location of where I had seen the balloon. I wanted to get a better view of it and maybe get closer to it. I wondered if it could be a black balloon. I had seen giant balloons at a car dealership in Bend to get people's attention. First of all, there were no car dealerships in that part of town, and I had never seen a black balloon hanging in the skies before. Those balloons were blue, red, white, and any other color except black. Maybe there was another event with a giant balloon to get our attention.

I had noticed that the black balloon was not moving. It was utterly motionless, hanging there in front of me in the sky. Balloons normally move. This one felt stationary.

I had kept the location of that black circle very tight in my memory. I then turned back to the direction where I had seen the balloon. I expected it to be there again in my vision, but that didn't happen. It was gone. I slowed down and took a detailed look at all possible locations where it could have moved. There was nothing to be seen. It was gone. I had an excellent view of the open sky now, and no black balloon or any other object was to be found by me in the sky.

I felt very frustrated; it should have been there. I saw it before. There had been only a short time-lapse where I could not view that location and where I had seen it before. Now it was gone - vanished.

I tried to figure out what had happened. Did I see that? Yes, I saw this black balloon/circle. It was right there in the sky I assured myself. What could it have been; why was it gone now and where did it go? I had many questions.

I still do not have answers, but I have my ideas. It could have been a UFO that had clocked itself as a black sphere. Maybe it wasn't meant to be seen by me, but I did notice the black rounds sphere. By the time I had to turn the corners, it was gone, or at least I could not perceive it anymore.

Clocking technology exists.

18. Animal Communication and Telepathy

Figure 43 Paul communicating with deer

Figure 44 Mieke communicating with puppies

I feel deeply connected with animals, especially with dogs and cats. I can feel into them, and I know they can feel into me. I can talk to them, and they can talk to me. I could improve my listening skills a little more. I have a busy mind, and to listen deeply, I have to quiet my mind and connect with my heart. A life-long work in progress!

Animals represent unconditional love. They know who they are and know they are love. Because of that, I often feel more at ease in the presence of an animal, and I can allow myself to be more open-hearted. I know they are not judging me for who I am, what I think, and do.

Sometimes at night, in my dreams, when my conscious mind is not in control, animals have come to me with messages. Also, diseased animals have shared some valuable information in my dreams. I am always grateful when that happens.

We humans, animals, and other species are all connected telepathically. That telepathic connection stays forever if we are consciously aware of it or not. We are always connected, alive or not.

18.1. Fourth of July Fireworks.

My Golden Retriever, Rayca, was my soft furry child and companion when I lived in Belgium. When I moved to the US in 1999, he, of course, moved with me. Paul and his three children also had a dog named Beauregard.

Figure 45 Beauregard

On July 4, 2002, a colleague invited us to her house for a 4th of July party. We had left the dogs home with the screen door open for fresh air. Beauregard had been shot in the leg as a puppy and was terrified of the sounds of the fireworks.

When we arrived home early evening, we noticed Rayca sitting next to the damaged screen door right before sunset. Beauregard had escaped through the screen door and ran away. We were not able to find him. We drove around the neighborhood, asking around if anyone had seen him. No luck. We called him and called him. I used my intuition and tried to connect with him telepathically. Night fell. We had to give up the search and go home. With a sad and worried heart and mind, we went to bed. I asked Beauregard to connect with me in my sleep and tell me where he was.

He did appear in my dreams. I saw him. I noticed a fragile, energetic cord between him and the organs of his body. It barely connected his organs with his soul. Then I woke up. Because of what my dream showed me, I knew he was in the process of dying or maybe was already dead.

131

As soon as the morning light appeared, I got up and got in the car. I drove around the neighborhood looking for Beauregard. He had contacted me, which gave me the motivation to search and hope that I could find him. I called his name out loud and asked people around.

Then I noticed a woman outside her house. I stopped, got out of the car, and asked if she had seen a sizeable blond dog. I explained what had happened. She confirmed she had seen a larger-sized blond dog on the side of the road not far from our home. Someone must have stopped and put a blanket under him because she noticed he was lying on a blanket, most likely dead.

I knew it was Beauregard. I could feel it. I thanked her and quickly drove to where she had seen the dog. There he was - our beloved Beauregard laying on a soft red blanket on the side of the road - dead.

I felt a huge relief. Relief because we found Beauregard and knew now where he was. Relief that someone had treated our dog lovingly by providing a blanket. Knowing he must have felt that love and respect as he was making his transition. I felt gratitude for the fact that Beau had contacted me in my dreams that night and had shown and informed me that he was barely hanging on to his life and his physical body. That message had told me that he was dying or already had died. He had been able to reach me, and I received his consciousness.

I am very thankful for being open to receiving telepathic messages, messages in my dreams, intuitive messages, and communications with those in the afterlife. I know we all have this ability. We do not always remember we do or learn how to use or activate and reclaim our innate abilities.

18.2. My dog Rayca and I are one

Figure 46 Rayca 1994-2003

Rayca, my Golden Retriever, was born in 1994. The veterinarian told me Rayca had an enlarged heart when he was a puppy. He also had frequent epileptic seizures during his life. He then lost control over his body and started shaking violently.

Rayca was nine years old in 2003. I had been noticing that his health was declining. He showed signs of being old and tired of being in his body.

One day unexpectedly, I found Rayca lying down in the grass in front of our house and unable to move his body. I tried to guide him up, but he was not able to. I looked into his eyes and saw his consciousness was alive and clear and aware. He looked at me, and I looked at him. I noticed his body had given up, but his soul was alive and well and awake. I wasn't sure what was going on.

I told Paul, let's put him in the car and drive him to the vet. I felt so much love for Rayca. I felt our connection; our hearts were so close. We left the kids at home and told them to stay with our other dog, named Love, and wait until we returned. I had no idea when we left the house that the kids would never see Rayca again. If I knew, I would have taken them to the vet as well.

Rayca could not move anymore, so we carried him on a blanket into the car and then into the vet's office. The vet looked at Rayca. At that moment, I realized it was time to let him go - my dear beautiful baby. My friend and companion with whom I had so many beautiful experiences. He was my guiding light in transitioning from my life in Belgium to the USA. He was my soulmate and support system. Paul and the children also loved him so much. He had touched the hearts of many people around the world. He lived in Belgium, Oregon, and Hawaii.

As he was lying there on the blanket, and before the vet could explain what was going on, I knew I had to say my goodbyes and let him go. I looked at Paul and said, "Paul, we have to let him go. He is ready. He does not want to go on anymore in this body." It was a shocking moment for Paul. Neither of us expected this. At that moment, I knew. Rayca was telling me he was ready. I heard him. I wanted to do what he wanted to do. There was no reason to hang on. I looked in his eyes, and he looked in mine. I told him I loved him so much. I hugged him and cried my tears onto his soft golden hair.

I think I was more prepared to let him go than Paul was. Paul and I looked at each other and Rayca, and both agreed. We cried and hugged him close to our hearts. We told Rayca he could go. When we were ready, the vet came into the room. We sang to Rayca as the vet gave him an injection to help him transition.

What happened next took me totally by surprise!

When the vet gave the first injection, I felt Rayca leaving his body. His soul energy came right into me. I could feel him entering my energy field. It was as if Rayca had been a part of me expressed outside myself as my dog. And that outer part was returning to me. Suddenly, I felt one with him, as if our two separate identities were reunited harmoniously into one whole gain. It was an unusual and very empowering experience. It took me entirely by surprise. The sadness that I had to let Rayca go immediately replaced with an inner feeling of expansion and completion within myself.

For Paul, it was also a profoundly moving experience. Paul felt a deep sadness.

Here are Paul's words about his connection with Rayca.

When I first met Rayca, I knew he was a beautiful, sensitive being with a big heart and a playful disposition. In the days and years that we traveled and lived together as a family, I grew closer and closer to him. I had been with him as he had experienced several seizures before. He had always recovered after a time, usually after he could relax and calm his body and nervous system.

This time was different. It was Rayca's time to go on to other adventures in other realities. I did not want him to leave yet as he had become a very dear companion. It took me a long time to realize that he wanted and needed to let his physical body go. Tears welled up in my eyes, and an aching arose in my heart. I sent him love and Reiki to help him on his journey, but the sadness and sense of grief remained with me for a long time. I often remember him as this noble being with clear soft brown eyes who shared so much with Mieke, our three kids, and me.

I understood Paul's deep sense of pending loss. I was confused that this was a positive experience for me and not a sad one. I was also relieved knowing that Rayca was not carrying his old diseased earthly body around anymore and could move freely in spirit form.

I was concerned for the children that we had to return home without Rayca. If I had known that they would never see him again in his physical body, I would have taken all kids with us to the vet. I shared with the children my experience, how I felt Rayca's energy return inside me and made me feel more whole. Paul, too, shared with them his deep emotional experience. We showed the children that it is natural to have unique emotional experiences around death and the subject of dying.

18.3. Telepathic communication with our dog named Love.

Figure 47 Love, Oregon

Our newest adopted puppy, Love was found abandoned on an Indian reservation. Some horseback riders had seen her trying to drink water from a broken bottle. She was pregnant and starving. They took her with them with the intent to find a good home for her. She picked us by jumping into Paul's lap and giving him a wet-loving lick, and we had no other choice than to take her in. She was very skittish and terrified when we first got her, sensitive and powerful at the same time.

One night I was sleeping, and Love was with me in the room. Suddenly, I saw in my mind's eye while asleep that she was sitting in a sphinx position next to my bed, intensely looking at me. She had penetrated my mind.

That penetration got my attention. It woke me up, and I opened my eyes. I looked next to my bed, and Love was sitting there precisely as I had seen in my mind's eye in sphinx position, looking intently at me.

I immediately knew what was happening. I understood what Love was telling me. She wanted to go out. We lived outside of Bend, Oregon, on 70 acres, and our dog was free to roam outdoors. Maybe she needed to pee badly, or she heard something outside and wanted to check it out. I got the message! She tried to get my attention to open the door for her. What a powerful telepathic experience that was for me.

Our dogs and cats communicate with us all the time. They converse in pictures. If I learned to quiet my mind more often, it would be easier to receive what they share with me. Paul understands this phenomenon better as he also receives information in pictures. I am learning to master that innate ability better as well.

Figure 48 Love on Pilot Butte, Bend, Oregon

Figure 49 Love living a free life on 70 acres in Bend, Oregon

18.4. We Love Animals

Figure 50 Gauthier, Love, Rayca and Leen

Figure 51 Love and Gauthier, Bandon, Oregon

Figure 52 Paul and Love

Figure 53 Kids and puppies

19. Flying a UFO - Transporting Metals

I consciously recall two instances where I was flying a UFO myself. In the first instance, I was transporting metals.

The UFO I was flying was my own. I was the pilot and the only person in the craft. I was about to fly to Earth to transport metals but wasn't 100% sure if going by myself this time was the best idea. I had a feeling that it might be better to have someone with me.

I remember approaching a little beach. A young boy around the age of five, which I knew, was playing in the sand. I stopped my craft in mid-air. While still in my vehicle, I approached the boy at the beach.

I mentioned to him that I was going to Earth transporting metals and asked him if he was interested in going with me this time around - a routine job I had done many times. Also, the little boy was familiar with my mission.

I waited for the little boy's reply. It was as a simple question as I would ask my child, "Hey, I am going to the store. Would you like to go with me or stay home?" The little boy kept playing in the sand while I asked my question. Without looking up at me, he responded, "sure." He decided to join me.

Afternote:

This experience happened in 1998 when I was still living in Belgium. I moved to the US in 1999.

In 2001, my sister's son was born in Belgium. When he visited us in the US for the second time at the age of five, I recognized his energy as the little boy on the beach who decided to go with me to Earth to transport the metals.

I believe that our earthly relationships exist and expand beyond time and space.

20. Flying a UFO - Observing Jupiter

I consciously recall a second instance where I was flying a UFO. This time I was observing the planet Jupiter.

I was flying the craft. One colleague was assisting me on this mission.

Both of us were standing behind the large control panel in the middle of the navigation room. This switchboard was facing the large to the top out rounding clear window. That window provided a stunning outlook on the cosmos and its star systems.

I stood on the left facing the window; my colleague was standing on my right. Our craft was hanging motionless in space. We had an excellent view of the undeniably impressive deep dark cosmos through the window. Observing the vastness of this dark essence, I felt absolute silence and the aliveness of the galaxy all at once. It was a breathtaking observation outside of me, and at the same time, I felt part of it and connected to it all.

Looking through the window, the giant planet of Jupiter was right in front of us. Its colors contrast with the deep dark space were tangible and explicit. Jupiter was hanging in the darkness distinctly tilted to the left.

Our mission was to observe the planet Jupiter. That was precisely our task. While our craft was stationary in front of the planet, we had an impeccable perspective at the perfect and precise distance to do our observations. We then logged all details and information into the control panel.

Both of us were highly knowledgeable and suited for this mission and felt very comfortable with the task at hand. Our teamwork was indisputable. We applied our knowledge, focused our attention on the job at hand, examined our observations, and contemplated what we discovered.

The all-powerful dynamic soul of the planet Jupiter was palpable. The planet was alive and conscious just as we were. There was respect for each other's spirit and presence. Our teamwork wasn't only between my colleague and me. Jupiter and the two of us worked together on this vital mission.

21. He Vanished Before my Eyes!

The store I was working at was hiring a new store director, and three candidates were applying for the open position. All three of them would be visiting the store on the same day. As employees, we were encouraged to talk to the three candidates and ask them questions. It was a great way to get to know them, their work style, and their views. We had a chance to share what we were looking for in a store director and ask them how they would take on specific needs in our department and store. It is a beautiful way to get a sense of who they are, and which candidate would best fit our store. Afterward, we were encouraged to honestly share our opinions and conclusions about the three candidates with the other teams. Every employee in our store had a chance to be involved in this crucial decision-making. I appreciated this opportunity to be included and have my voice heard.

On the day of the visit, I was working. When noticing the first candidate, I took the opportunity to connect and ask my questions. I immediately had a good feeling about this person. He seemed to be himself and honest. I related with him spontaneously and authentically. He answered my questions well, and I sensed that his personality and previous experiences would benefit our store. For me, this first candidate was a "yes" so far. Eagerly, I waited to meet and get to know the other two candidates.

Later that morning as I walked towards my department, I saw the second candidate. Alright, I thought, this is my chance to talk to number two.

I introduced myself and asked him a question about my department. We were standing face to face in front of each other. While he answered my question, I blinked my eyes and he was gone. He had vanished in front of me in mid-sentence. I quickly looked around wondering where he could have gone. I looked in all directions. There could not have been time for him even to walk away. I had just blinked my eyes, and by the time I opened them again he was gone.

This was strikingly unusual and weird. A few seconds before I started a conversation and an eye blinked later, I stood there all by myself. Again, I contemplated all options where he could have walked away in that tiny blink of an eye. There was no place for him to have disappeared behind a shelf or a pole. The nearest shelf was further away, and the pillar I was standing near was still too far out for him to have moved behind it. It was mind-boggling that we had just started our conversation and were literally in mid-sentence. No one else was around. Nothing made sense! This whole situation was remarkably unusual.

I stood there perplexed and wondered if he would return. After a while, I sensed this would not be the case. It felt weird; he abandoned me in mid-sentence. There was no trace left of him. I felt ridiculous just standing there. Because I thought he was fooling me, I decided to keep walking towards my department. I kept looking around to see if I could detect him somewhere in the store, but I did not. I looked around for the rest of my shift, hoping to further observe his actions. I did not see him again that day.

This experience was uncool. In that moment that I did connect, I did not have a good feeling about this guy. When comparing the two candidates I'd met, candidate one for sure had my vote so far. I didn't want this disappearing, ill-feeling second candidate to be our next store director.

That same day, I asked around if other people had talked to candidate number two. I thought maybe someone else had noticed anything unusual. Only one person I asked said yes. When I asked what her experience was with this person, her response was, "he seems nice, but they all seem nice." This feedback didn't give me valuable input in my investigation.

This experience had put me on guard and activated my curiosity. Something was not right, I knew. I could not understand what happened here. The first candidate had felt normal, but something was totally off with the second one. The third one never showed up that day. It was clear that the one who did disappear on me was not the one I would choose as a store director. But guess what - that was precisely the one that got the position!

I was disappointed. Does it have to be the second one? I thought to myself. As he arrived on the job, I observed him. I didn't immediately talk to him. I wanted to sense and figure out who he was. Something didn't feel right. My intuition told me to watch and observe how he interacted with others and how he behaved in his position. My solar plexus rang very loud; I call it my bullshit detector. Pay attention and stay away it said.

As the days, weeks and months unfolded, I tried to connect and did my best to create a working relationship with him. Repeatedly I felt that something wasn't right. In my mind, I revisited that first initial contact with him and the fact that he had disappeared on me in mid-sentence. My mind tried to rationalize the situation, and I wanted to convince myself that there must have been a logical reason for what had happened. But still, I felt something was off.

And then guess what? A few months later, it happened again. I walked upstairs towards the copy machine located right in front of the store director's office. Ready to make a copy, I put my paper in the copy machine, and I noticed that the store director was walking out of his office towards me. I looked at him, acknowledged his presence, and said hi. As I look at him, he replied hi, and he vanishes again in front of my eyes!

He was gone again in less than a second as I was standing there right in front of him. I quickly looked around and checked his office to see if he had walked back in there. I checked the office right next to the copy machine. I checked the stairs to see if he was maybe walking down. I checked all spaces around me. I was much quicker in responding now because this was the second time this had happened to me. The first time I had no idea what had just happened. This second time, I was more prepared! My initial response was shock again. But then I quickly considered all options and checked all possible logical spaces he could have retreated. Nothing! He was gone again—I found no trace.

Now I knew for sure there was something undoubtedly unusual going on. Our store director had disappeared in front of my eyes for the second time while in conversation while connecting.

I had heard about shape-shifters and cloaking techniques, but mostly from movies and stories. I knew that I was dealing with a phenomenon I couldn't understand. But how do I share this experience with others? And with who? How do I explain what just happened? Everyone would run this story through their logical mind and would question mine. Who would believe me? This mystery was not the first unusual experience in my life.

While attempting to understand, I came up with a few possible explanations. This man cloaked himself, jumped into another dimension, shape-shifted, or time jumped. I do not understand how that works, but I figured he did something on purpose. Maybe he was enjoying messing with my mind.

After that second experience, I questioned other colleagues even more about their experiences and interactions with him. I asked if they had noticed any unusual things? I received two kinds of responses from people—one type of response from those who didn't trust him, including me. And a different kind of response from those who said they liked him, which I found to be the people who wanted to be appreciated by him because he was the store director in a position of power.

Because of these experiences, it was a bizarre time for me. I was always on guard going to work. I didn't trust him. I didn't like what I felt when in his presence or interacting with him. I also thought that he was checking out who I was. And that he could sense that I wasn't going to let myself be intimidated by him. I kept my "energetic" ground.

And then it happened again, a third time. As I was helping in the vitamin department. I saw the store director walk by, and again, he vanished in front of my eyes as I was looking at him. This time we were not in conversation. I knew then for sure something was up. This person was not a normal human being. There was more to him. Because I had experienced it three times, I trusted my initial, intuitive impressions. After a few years working with him, I realized that he didn't feel like a normal heart-based human being. He didn't feel good to me. I also noticed other things that activated my bullshit detector, which gave me more information about who and what I was dealing with here.

He had two sons around the ages of five and seven. Those kids looked drained, white in their face, reserved, scared, and not happy. It felt to me that their dad sucked up their life force energy. I felt concerned for those kids and wondered what was going on with them privately.

One day, another intuitive alarm bell went off. I worked in the bakery right next to the kitchen area. It was later in the afternoon, between the lunch and dinner rush and only three other employees were working in the kitchen. One was the kitchen manager, who had by now become a friend of mine. I noticed the store director enter the kitchen area. Suddenly, he pulls a picture out of his pocket and shows it to one of the three employees. She screamed out loud and said, "that is horrible!" I could feel her horrific response when witnessing that picture. The second employee approached him to see for herself what was in the picture. He showed her the image, and she reacted in horror and despair. The manager also asked to see the picture and expressed deep repulsion. She kept repeating, "that is horrible and disgusting," and ordered him to put it away. "How can you do that to us? Put that picture way", she demanded him. He enjoyed their reaction. I could feel the fear that the picture had triggered in all three of them. While they showed anxiety, he got a big smile on his face. He enjoyed shocking them. I just stood there observing the situation. I was not interested in seeing the picture or being pulled into his vampirism power and fear games.

I didn't respond at all; I just observed. Then the store director left. I asked the kitchen manager what was on the picture. She said it looked like a pile of cut limbs and cut-open people. She was still feeling disgusted as she talked about it to me. In my opinion, he was harvesting the energy of their fear. He enjoyed it. Again, it was a confirmation and more explanation of who he was. A normal human being wouldn't do that.

It was very challenging for me to have him around at work. I was constantly on guard because I knew I was not dealing with an average person. After several years of observing and holding my ground and distance, I noticed he manipulated the employees. Typically, most people working in a corporate structure want to climb the ladder. They want to be recognized and loved by their bosses. That is a normal human inclination. We are herd animals, and we like to be included and loved by the herd especially those who seem to be leading the pack.

I heard employees sharing stories about parties he hosted where lots of alcohol and other drugs were involved. Many wanted to be part of those parties and be included by him.

After a few years, I noticed he was not at work, as mentioned on the schedule. He came and went as it pleased him. Because he could, he had the authority to do so and he did.

It was mind-boggling to me that someone with such behavior could stay in such a high position and get away with all of it without being called upon it. Then one day, the human resource department came in to ask about his behavior. I honestly shared that I didn't think he fit the position. I did not share my experiences with his disappearing on me because they would not comprehend it. The human resources department did not do anything about it, and he stayed in his position.

Paul and I felt that our time living in that area in Oregon was ending. It had been a great place to raise our children. Now that our two oldest children had finished high school, we decided it was our time to move on. There were several reasons we wanted to move away from the town. The situation with the store director was one of them.

In 2010, I transferred to another store in the chain in Santa Rosa in California. I felt relieved not to encounter that store director's energy anymore. It has always been a mystery why more employees did not sense that things weren't normal with him and why they didn't speak up. He stayed for several more years in that same position in that store, until he decided to move on.

22. Meeting Travis Walton - Sonoma International Film Festival 2016

Figure 54 Mieke and Travis Walton

As residents of Santa Rosa, California, Paul and I learned about the Sonoma International Film Festival. It was 2016. I read in a newspaper that it was the sixth anniversary of the UFO symposium, a popular film-and-conversation event as part of the festival. This was the only annual UFO movie symposium to take place at an international film festival.

Figure 55 UFO-Jim Introducing the UFO Symposium

"Unidentified Flying Objects are the biggest, most important topic on the planet Earth," declared Jim Ledwith in the paper. Jim is a Sonoma-based "UFOlogist" and curator-founder of the annual UFO Symposium known to many by the nickname "UFO Jim." This year the UFO Symposium featured one of its most famous guests, Travis Walton.

Travis Walton of Arizona is best known as the subject of the 1993 film "Fire in the Sky", a Hollywood spin on Travis Walton's memoir detailing his alien abduction. His abduction took place in Arizona's remote Apache-Sitgreaves National Forest. Travis was working there with a forestry crew on November 5, 1975.

"Beings abducted him from space," says Jim Ledwith. "For five days, the authorities thought his co-workers had murdered him, and then he was returned. All of the co-workers who were there, who saw the spacecraft, they all took polygraph tests, and they all passed, except for one, and that one was inconclusive."

Along with a Friday night screening of "Fire in the Sky", the new documentary, "Travis: The True Story of Travis Walton" by Jennifer Stein, was to be presented and screened followed by a panel discussion featuring Travis Walton, Jennifer Stein, and others.

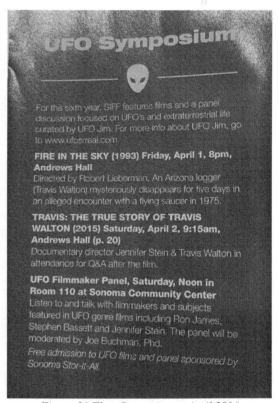

Figure 56 Flyer Symposium – April 2016

Jennifer Stein has often described her recollections of seeing something she believes is an alien spacecraft. "It was 1975," she explains in the paper, "the same year Travis was abducted. I was 19, and I was afraid to say anything about it for years. Eventually, I decided I could no longer stay in the dark, and so I decided to speak out and try to find a way to make a difference."

"Interest in UFOs is enormous. UFOs are the next big issue for humanity," Jennifer Stein explained further. Acknowledging that plenty of people remain unconvinced of the existence of aliens or UFOs, Jennifer invited them to come to see her film in Sonoma and stay after to give feedback. She said, "There is no issue more important to the future of the world and our species."

After reading the news article, I realized that Travis Walton and Jennifer Stein would be in Sonoma, only a half-hour drive from our home in Santa Rosa.

Even though Travis's experience was different from mine, I had never met another person who claimed to have had abduction experiences. I know how hard it is to come to terms with my own alien abduction experiences, let alone being able to talk about it in public. It intrigued me that Travis was able to do that. I wanted to meet this person. I wanted to have a first-hand experience of who he is, how he shared his experiences, and how he held himself while sharing. What does he think about his own experiences, how does he answer the questions about aliens and abductions? How does he feel now, and what motivates him to keep talking about his experiences?"

Paul and I bought tickets and looked forward to meeting Travis and hearing first-hand about his story and experiences.

On the first night of the symposium, we watched the movie "Fire in the Sky" on the big screen
followed by a Q&A. Travis came on stage and answered everyone's questions.

I had seen "Fire in the Sky" in my teenage years. I didn't consciously link the movie to my own abduction experiences at that time. I had most of those memories repressed and could hardly comprehend them myself.

156

Seeing the movie for a second time as an adult, I comprehended that the film was about Travis's real-life experience. It was apparent that Hollywood dramatized certain parts of the movie. Nevertheless, the story was out for the public to see, and that was a huge step forward in informing and educating the public.

As I watched the movie, I observed Travis sitting in the front row. He was sitting there in his chair quietly and calmly watching the movie. I was curious to see what he thought about it now.

After the movie, Travis answered questions for a long time. He appeared to me as a quiet and humble person. It became evident that Travis wasn't doing this event for his pleasure or aggrandizement. That is not who he is as a person. It felt that if Travis had a choice, this would not be what he would choose to do with his life. The experience happened. I believe he felt the responsibility to share what he experienced and how this event has affected his life and all those participants around him. I think he wants to be honest with the world and bring the truth out.

On the second day of the symposium, we were eager to see Jennifer Steins new documentary, "Travis - The True Story of Travis Walton."

Before the showing, Jennifer and Travis came on stage and introduced themselves and the documentary. Jennifer explained, "The documentary was five years in the making. The true story had never been told in a documentary". "I believed the time had come to capture these interviews and testimonies on film for the next generation before the next dis-informant arrives trying to debunk the facts again, as has happened so many times in the past," she said.

"Hopefully, this film accomplished its goal to recognize all the members of this logging crew and their experiences which have been equally as difficult as the challenges Travis Walton has faced. The film is a personal interest story into how this event challenged their lives and changed their lives forever," Jennifer said.

Jennifer acknowledged the bravery of Travis and his fellow logging crew members, who could have easily denied this story because of the negative media attention they received for decades. They could have saved themselves from years of ridicule and claimed it was all a hoax, but they never have yet. They all stuck to the truth of their story for 40 years despite the ridicule they endured.

Figure 57 Jennifer & Travis sharing about the Documentary

After this introduction, I was even more intrigued and ready to view this documentary. I felt grateful to have the opportunity to meet Travis and Jennifer in person and follow their journey of bringing out their truth to the world; a truth and topic that has been suppressed and derided in our current society. I knew from my own experiences that what he had experienced and shared was true. I knew because I had lived it myself in my own way. Meeting him now in person made my experiences even more valid.

The lights went off, and the documentary started on the big screen. Paul and I watched intently. I used my intuition and observed every detail presented in the documentary. I compared my own experience and reactions with the reactions and testimony of Travis and his crew.

The documentary was about a 40-year history of events resulting from the startling UFO encounter in 1975, which forever changed the lives of the seven loggers.

It documented the years of sworn testimony, multiple polygraph examinations, numerous specialists looking at this data over decades, along with physical evidence. All of this provides the preponderance of evidence enabling this case to be considered one of the most significant UFO cases ever.

The documentary featured all living members of the original logging crew, including current and archived interviews woven together, the police, sheriff, and the chief polygraph expert for Arizona in 1975. It also contained UFO expert presentations by Stanton Friedman, Richard Dolan, Kathleen Marden, Linda Moulton Howe, Ben Hansen, James Fox, Peter Robbins, and Lee Spiegel.

Paul and I found this documentary incredibly well put together and presented. It was so much more realistic and convincing than the Hollywood version. It was the truth, the real deal.

The audience very well received the documentary. There was a standing ovation. Jennifer and her lead film editors, Adam Stein and Zachary Weil, had done an incredible job!

The feeling I had was one of gratitude. Gratitude for Travis's bravery, for everyone who was affected, their willingness to tell their truth, and stay in their integrity.

This documentary was an invaluable gift to us. I was able to hear the witnesses and participants speak their truth. I saw the length they went to prove their truth. Their lives had taken a whole different turn than what their lives would have been without this event.

It motivated us to share about our own UFO and alien contact experiences. In 1975 the world was not ready to receive these truths. The time is ripe now for sharing more openly. Disclosure is growing in acceptance. The cover-up and lies are getting exposed. Because of that, we feel secure and ready to contribute our part and share what we have lived.

After the showing of the documentary, Travis and Jennifer held another Q&A. They invited everyone to come back the next day for a panel interview with Travis, Jennifer, and others and ask our questions.

I felt so much more informed and at ease with myself after seeing the two screenings and having met Jennifer and Travis in person. The way they presented themselves, the film, and the documentary, and how they interacted with the audience was proof of their authenticity. They were just simply able to be themselves. That was THE reason why we were there, to find this out and to determine our path forward.

The panel interview the next day was at the Sonoma Community Center. Paul and I sat in the front row on the left. I always prefer sitting in front. I can feel the speakers better, and I do not get distracted by people in front of me.

Figure 58 Panel Interview

Figure 59 Travis Walton

The people on the panel were Travis Walton, Jennifer Stein, Stephen Bassett, Ron James, and the moderator, Joe Buckman. I was able to ask my questions and talk to Travis and Jennifer in person after the panel. Jennifer and Travis encouraged us to start sharing our own experiences.

Figure 60 Jennifer Stein and Mieke

Astronaut Edgar Mitchell and longtime friend of producer Jennifer Stein wrote an impressive endorsement for the film.

Since the premiere of this film, it has appeared in 28 mainstream film festivals. This definitive documentary is now available on Amazon with subtitles in French, Italian, Spanish, Japanese, and English for the hearing impaired.

We strongly recommend this documentary to anyone interested in or with questions about this phenomenon.

Afternote:

I believe that Travis' abduction experience is of a different nature than what I experienced. It seems to me that Travis' curiosity was a little naive when he jumped out of the car and approached the glowing craft that was taking off. He was in the wrong place at the wrong time. The craft was leaving and transmitted a strong force, possibly an electromagnetic force that lifted him off the ground and threw him through the air, leaving him unconscious on the ground. I think that the E.T.'s realized he was injured and took him on board to help him heal from the force field event. When the healing process was completed they brought him back in an area where he could safely be reunited with his family. I believe that those onboard were benevolent.

Jennifer Stein's Website https://onwingesproductions.com/

Travis Walton The Movie https://traviswaltonthemovie.com/

Figure 61 E.T. Welcoming Paul

Figure 62 E.T. Welcoming Mieke

23. In Paul's Words

Figure 63 Paul at Crater Lake, 2006

Figure 64 Paul in Hood River, 2019

Mieke and I were divinely guided; our lives collided together from two different cultures and two different generations. Nothing made logical sense. However, we both knew better and followed our hearts instead of logic. After we were married and lived together in Oregon, we learned more about each other and each other's lives. We realized that we both had our extraordinary, not often talked about experiences. Here are a few of my personal experiences that stood out for me in my life:

23.1 The Scissors

At age three and a half, I was in the kitchen of our first house on Tucker Road with my mom, Frances. She asked me if I had seen her sewing scissors in one instance. I said that I had seen her scissors. "I see them now," I said as I gazed into the living room - only there was a solid wall between me and the living room. I pointed at the scissors from my perspective though it appeared I was pointing at that wall saying, "right there, right there." My mom looked where I was indicating and exclaimed, "You can't see through walls!" And the wall flashed into solid existence, and the scissors vanished from my sight! I was shocked as was my mom! I have not seen through walls ever since!

23.2 First UFO Sighting

My first UFO sighting occurred in 1969 when I was 19 years old. One of my close friends and I were parked on a mountain road when we witnessed a light moving above a ridge near Mount Hood in Oregon. It moved horizontally from right to left from our perspective and relatively slowly. Then after observing it for about a couple of minutes, it suddenly shifted direction 90 degrees and disappeared as a streak of light in an instant - straight up.

23.3 Miracle on US-30

Later that year in 1969, I drove my car from Hood River to Portland on US-30. I was on my way to Corvallis and OSU (Oregon State University). It was a cold and misty fall day.

I approached a section where the road narrowed to two lanes to enter the tunnel near Bonneville. Visibility was poor due to fog.

Unexpectedly, I heard a voice clearly instruct, "Hit your brakes and veer left!" However, there was no one else in the car. I immediately complied. Brake! Veer!

Looking through the fog, I saw brake lights ahead. The cars were stopped. I aimed for the space between the guard rail and the stopped cars. I passed cars one, two, three, and a pickup too close to the guard rail to squeeze through. My vehicle stopped with several feet to spare! I was shaken.

It was a miracle! Some force had intervened, and I didn't hit the vehicles or the guard rail. Both my car and I were unscathed.

23.4 Two Beings Appear in My Dental Practice

As a practicing dentist in Oregon in 1979, I experienced a severe headache. I sent my office staff home, closed my office, and locked the doors. I lay down in my dental chair to rest before driving home. I was awakened by two beings in the room standing behind my dental chair.

When I questioned their presence, they announced, "We notice that you have a headache."

I acknowledged, "yes, a severe one, which I never have." They produced a device about 1.5 inches in diameter and 16 to 18 inches in length. They waved the device over my head from side to

169

side from behind me and said, "The reason you have a headache is because you have a brain tumor." I was dismayed but before I could talk, they explained, "This is not a problem, and after adjusting something on this device, they waved it over my head again from side to side several times and the headache disappeared. Then they said, "There, it's gone."

To my astonishment, the pain had completely disappeared! "This is amazing," I exclaimed! Where can I get one of those?" With my science and medical background, I immediately recognized the incredible value of such a device that could diagnose and reverse something as potentially devastating as a brain tumor in seconds.

They replied, "We will send you one." I asked where they lived, and they pointed straight up. That was shocking because there was nothing above my office but the roof and sky!

At that point, I dozed off, and when I awakened, the headache was still completely gone. The doors and windows were still locked, and the two individuals had vanished.

I am still waiting for this device to be delivered. Actually, I believe that this technology is already on our planet.

24. Sharing our Truth with Others

Carrying all those experiences within me and having no outlet to talk about or discuss those events during my earlier life has brought inner stress, insecurity, and an imbalance within myself. As a child, my few attempts to communicate those experiences with others were unsuccessful. I was not believed or even laughed at. What mostly stopped me from further attempts to share. When that part of me didn't find a place to express itself or be acknowledged, I put those experiences aside and suppressed them.

Luckily, the deep desire for truth and inner freedom stayed very strong in me. "Who am I and why I am here" those questions remained very present within my awareness. Looking for answers in the "then called occult" books in our bookstore and the local library was extremely helpful during my search. Attending alternative healing classes in Belgium and a geomancy class in the Netherlands supported my journey. It surrounded me with open-minded people who were also looking for answers to the truth of who we are as souls living a human life.

My intuition has always been strong, and I learned to act on it. When Divine intervention brought me to Paul and the children, I knew what I had to do.

After we got married, Paul and I discovered that we both had many out-of-the-ordinary experiences. Even if we didn't comprehend many of them, the fact that we had each other talk about it was a tremendous support. We trusted each other as a sounding board and support system. We joined forces on our search for truth and freedom. We discovered that we had the same purpose in life, "to live an honest, free, and inspired life."

I carried in me deep-seated fears and had many questions about those memories of alien abductions and other phenomena. Most of the experiences were benevolent and very powerful. Those that were fear-inducing were boggling my mind.

When we moved to California in 2010, I heard about Laurie Mc Donald's E.T. experiencers group in Sacramento. Every month she freely opened her home for E.T. experiencers to come together and share about what they have experienced. Even Sacramento was a 2.5-hour drive away from where we lived in Santa Rosa; I felt a strong pull for us to attend a gathering. I was nervous and felt emotionally stirred the first time we participated. This event was a new experience for us.

For the first time in our lives, Paul and I could openly and freely share with others what we had experienced. Our sharing was received well, and we were able to hear about the other people's experiences in the group.

I learned that it was safe and OK to talk about those experiences. A door I had previously closed was opening up for us. For the next few years, I processed many hidden emotions inside myself. I was making room in my life for those stored away experiences to have a place and be acknowledged: an internal process that takes time and lots of patience.

Sharing in an experiencers group's closed and safe environment was one step. Meeting Travis Walton and observing how he was openly and freely sharing his personal and deeply vulnerable experiences with the whole world was a second major step in my healing process. It gave us an extra boost of energy and motivation to open ourselves up to the world.

If Travis could share his truth with the world in such a humble and honest way, at least we could start this process as well, Paul and I concluded. We didn't know yet how and with who we would share. We felt inspired and decided to first open up about our experiences with open-minded and interested friends. The new documentary about Travis made by Jennifer Stein was such a rich tool to start a conversation. I asked Jennifer herself if we could use her documentary to open a discussion with others, and she strongly recommended going for it and creating our unique ways of sharing with the world.

In our living room in Santa Rosa, we invited interested friends. After watching the documentary together, we shared some of our own experiences, opened the floor for questions and answers, and discussed the topic.

During those first initial gatherings, when sharing about the traumatic abduction experiences, I could feel the deeper stored emotions bubbling up. I was processing them as I spoke my truth. Bringing those deep-kept and hidden emotional experiences back to the surface and back to light was a powerful and necessary process. The more I shared, the more I felt I was re-balancing myself.

Speaking my truth provided a healing process, an inner journey of learning to take responsibility in my life. Those parts of me that felt victimized and not understood were recognized, held in love, and transformed this way.

Since we shared our experiences with friends in our living room in Santa Rosa, we have ventured out and shared our truths with many others crossing our paths. We have since participated in experiencers meetings all around the world. Some were in-person gatherings and some online zoom meetings. We are now writing down what we have experienced and learned from it and we are sharing our stories through the several projects we are creating. Writing this book is one of them.

We intend to live a free, inspired, honest, and creative life and assist others in doing the same. In doing so, we are co-creating a free and inspired world where further generations will benefit from.

Figure 65 Mieke and Love in front of our Tipi

Figure 66 Paul, Christopher and Andrew, Bend, 2005

Figure 67 At home in Bend, Oregon

Figure 68 Paul and Christopher replacing an engine

Figure 69 Paul and Frank Coppieters

Figure 70 Mount Hood. Mieke's favorite mountain

Figure 71 Paul and Christopher 2004

Figure 72 Mieke and Christopher

Figure 73 Paul and Mieke 2016

Figure 74 Andrew, Mieke, Christopher, Angela and Paul in Orval, Belgium 2015

Acknowledgments

Paul Benton, Karen Viscuso, Desta Barnabe, Brenda Seals, Matt Lacasse, for assisting with the editing, publishing, and cover of the book.

Biography

Mieke Benton was born in 1970 in the city of Gent, Belgium. From a very young age, she had extraordinary experiences that others didn't seem to talk or know about. Questions such as who am I and why am I here guided her on the path of alternative healing, geomancy, UFO investigations, inter-dimensional realities, consciousness expansion, mind control, universal awareness, and more. At age 27, through Divine intervention, she met Paul and his then three young children in an international alternative healing retreat in Breitenbush Hotsprings, Oregon. The many unexpected synchronicities did not make any logical sense to them, being from two different cultures and two different generations. Finally, they couldn't ignore those interventions any longer, and it became undoubtedly clear that they were meant to be together. Mieke moved with her Golden Retriever to Hood River, Oregon, to start their new life together. After they married, Paul and Mieke realized they had both extraterrestrial and other unusual experiences and felt guided to share their journeys and lessons learned with the world.

Figure 75 Paul & Mieke 2016

181

Made in the USA
Columbia, SC
09 October 2024